Successful Com

Outreach

A How-To-Do-It Manual for Librarians®

Barbara Blake
Robert S. Martin
and Yunfei Du

HOW-TO-DO-IT MANUALS®

NUMBER 157

Neal-Schuman Publishers, Inc.
New York London

Published by Neal-Schuman Publishers, Inc.
100 William St., Suite 2004
New York, NY 10038
http://www.neal-schuman.com

Printed and bound in the United States of America.

The paper used in this publication meets the minimum requirements of American National Standard for Information Sciences—Permanence of Paper for Printed Library Materials, ANSI Z39.48-1992.

ISBN: 978-55570-772-9

Contents

List of Worksheets

Preface

Successful Community Outreach: A How-To-Do-It Manual for Librarians is intended to provide public library managers, leaders, and administrators with a set of tools and a process for developing effective community outreach plans. These plans will enable libraries to develop partnerships for addressing issues and resolving problems in the community, thereby embedding the library in the community, demonstrating its value, and strengthening the library as an essential part of community life.

This how-to manual covers the full range of a community outreach process, from identifying and defining the community frame of reference and articulating the role of the library in the community, to assessing the needs and assets in the community, to identifying potential programs and partners, through developing full-scale action plans and assessing their effectiveness. By following the process outlined in this manual, librarians will be able to develop a community outreach plan tailored to the specific characteristics, needs, and interests of their own community.

The tools and worksheets provided in the manual and on the accompanying CD-ROM support a step-by-step process that has been used successfully in many libraries. Examples of real problems, programs, and partners are provided.

Chapter 1 provides a brief introduction to community outreach and the planning process. Chapter 2 details how to begin the process by defining and describing the library and the community it serves. Chapter 3 will help planners determine the community's outreach needs and how to assess and approach potential programs and partners. Chapter 4 covers writing the plan itself. Throughout all four chapters, "IN & OUT" sidebars highlight tips for doing outreach projects held "in" and "out" of the library. These tell how to do the outreach program in the library if that is the best location for it because the library has the necessary resources (meeting room, computer lab, etc.) or out of the library if an off-site location is better. Most show how to do it both ways to help librarians think of ways to take things they have traditionally done in the library out into the community. Chapters 2, 3, and 4 also include a total of 24 worksheets that accompany each stage of plan development. The companion CD-ROM includes all 24 of these in Microsoft Word and PDF formats so that individual libraries can easily complete them as is or adapt them to meet their own needs.

Two appendixes are included to facilitate easier plan development. Appendix 1 lists Internet sources of community and demographic data that will inform library planning; live links to each source are also replicated on the CD-ROM for quicker access. Appendix 2 lists the seven completed outreach plans. The full text of all seven is available on the companion CD-ROM so readers can see what finished plans look like.

The book concludes with an extensive bibliography on community outreach that provides sources of further information.

This manual had its origins in a project developed by and carried out at the University of North Texas College of Information. The Promoting and Enhancing the Advancement of Rural Libraries (PEARL) project was initiated in the fall of 2010 with support from the Robert and Ruby Priddy Charitable Trust of Wichita Falls, Texas. When it is completed, the three-year PEARL project will have assisted approximately 105 targeted rural libraries to create a Community Outreach Plan and train library staff in the use of the plan. In carrying out the work of the project, a training manual on developing community outreach plans was drafted by the staff of the project. Although the manual was focused on libraries in a rural setting, it was readily apparent that the tools, forms, and process provided by the manual could easily be implemented by public libraries in any community setting. This book is the result.

Although *Successful Community Outreach: A How-To-Do-It Manual for Librarians* was principally designed for public libraries, the tools and processes it provides are easily adapted to other settings. School and academic libraries could utilize the community outreach process developed here to enhance their relations with and service to the communities they serve.

Acknowledgments

The authors wish to convey their gratitude to the Robert and Ruby Priddy Trust for its generous support of the PEARL project and for its interest in strengthening rural public libraries. Without the Trust there would have been no PEARL project, and consequently no community outreach planning manual. We are confident that both the project and this resulting manual will justify the faith that the Trust has placed in us.

The authors also wish to thank Dr. Herman L. Totten, Dean of the University of North Texas College of Information, for his leadership and support of the PEARL project. Without Dr. Totten's persistence at the outset, there probably would not have been a PEARL project. His vision and leadership have been indispensible in developing and carrying out this good work.

Finally, the authors would like to thank the participants in the first cohort of the PEARL project. These dedicated librarians from small and rural libraries in west Texas have invested their time and energy, often in the face of great obstacles, to make their libraries more effective agencies in advancing community life. The feedback that they have provided has enhanced the utility of this manual and will therefore serve as aid to countless other librarians in communities across the country.

Introduction

Public libraries face tremendous challenges. Rapidly evolving information technology enables access to ever-increasing forms of information and knowledge but presents enormous difficulties in terms of affordability, staff and user training, and rapid obsolescence. Shifting demographics, including rapidly aging and increasingly multicultural communities of users, require increasingly diverse resources and programs and lead to increased demand from social and civic service organizations that are attempting to meet the needs of their clients. Declining tax bases in many communities threaten library budgets and increase competition for scarce resources.

To confront and overcome these challenges successfully, libraries must create and demonstrate the value that they provide to the communities that they serve. The foundation for successful libraries lies in ensuring that libraries create public value. If the library is underappreciated as a community asset, and disadvantaged in competing for scarce community resources, it is often because the library is not viewed as an essential element in community life. The goal of the library in such situations should be to overturn that perception of the library, to strengthen the library as an essential element of community life. That goal is best accomplished by demonstrating the value of the library to the social leaders, elected officials, and resource allocators in the community.

The value that a library produces for its community is not determined by the library, its leaders, staff, and supporters. Public value is determined by the consumers of the library's services and must be responsive to their needs, interests, and desires. If we want to offer services that the public will value and support, it is imperative that we listen carefully and systematically to our elected officials and resource allocators to understand fully their agendas, their concerns, and their goals. We then need to take care to explain how libraries can help them achieve their goals and advance their agendas while at the same time responding to the needs of library users.

A key element in focusing on creating value is that we must evaluate programs and services and demonstrate their impact. We simply have to do a better job of demonstrating the value that we provide to the communities that we serve. This does not mean that we have to quantify everything—good stories are important too. The best kind of evaluation of outcomes is when the library is so enmeshed in its community that the community cannot imagine operating without it any more than it would operate without a police department or a fire department. The goal is to be perceived not as something nice to have but as something that is essential.

Of course, there is nothing new about focusing on creating and demonstrating value. In 1920, John Cotton Dana wrote:

> All public institutions . . . should give returns for their cost; and those returns should be in good degree positive, definite, visible, measurable. The goodness of a [library] is not in direct ratio to the cost of its building and the upkeep thereof, or to the rarity, auction value, or money cost of its collections. A [library] is good only insofar as it is of use. . . . Common sense demands that a publicly supported institution do something for its supporters and that some part at least of what it does be capable of clear description and downright valuation.[1]

One of the most successful ways to demonstrate a public value agenda is to develop a coalition or partnership around a particular issue or specific problem in the community. If you can broaden the base of supporters around an issue, you can often achieve success. These kinds of partnerships are essential. This kind of collaboration is aligned with how we are thinking about our communities as "holistic" environments, as social ecosystems in which we are part of an integrated whole. Collaboration is not a joined-at-the hip symbiosis, and it certainly is not a parasitic relationship. Instead, it is a mature and reflective recognition of intersecting nodes of interest, activity, and mission. It is the potential for creating synergy out of cooperation, building a structure in which the whole is greater than the sum of the parts. The goal of such collaborations is to be perceived not as an advocate for the library but rather as a player in the community, working with others to help solve community problems and advance the general welfare.

Libraries can work effectively to assist in resolving issues like early learning, economic development, child safety, family literacy, employment skills, and so many more. The objective, then, should be to identify the needs of the community, seek out partners in the community to work with in the community, and together develop a strategy and a plan for addressing that need. Every elected official has a set of priorities that needs to be addressed in the community, and the library can almost always find a way to assist and support those priorities. When the library demonstrates its value in this way, it will receive the appreciation and recognition it deserves and the resources it requires.

This manual is designed to provide an approach to demonstrating the value of the library. It provides a set of tools and processes to assist the leaders of any library in first, identifying and defining the community to be served; next, surveying the needs and assets of that community; and, then, identifying potential programs and partners to address those needs. Once these steps have been completed, this manual provides the framework for developing an effective plan, implementing the plan, and evaluating its success. Library leaders who follow the approach outlined in this manual, who use the tools and processes provided, will be able to develop and carry out successful projects, build effective community coalitions, and achieve the goal of strengthening the public library as an essential element of community life.

Note

1. Dana, John Cotton. 1916. "Increasing the Usefulness of Museums." Proceedings of the American Association of Museums 10. Reprinted in Dana, John Cotton. 1999. *The New Museum: Selected Writings of John Cotton Dana*, 101–102. Newark, NJ: The Newark Museum Association.

Describing the Library and Community

IN THIS CHAPTER:

- ✔ Library's Focus
- ✔ Community Profile
- ✔ Library Profile

Library's Focus

Having a library vision statement, mission statement, defined goals, measurable objectives, and detailed activities to accomplish your objectives are all necessary steps in determining the overall focus and direction of your library. It is important to have these planning elements in place to create an effective community outreach plan. Your plan for outreach activities should be developed within the context of your library's overall long-range plan.

Your library may have already created a long-range plan that includes the library's vision, mission, goals, and objectives. If so, you may find this section useful in reviewing and/or updating your long-range or strategic plan. Or you can just use your existing document to complete the worksheets included in this chapter. The information you put in these worksheets will be used later in Chapters 3 and 4.

If you do not have a written long-range plan for your library that includes each of the planning components mentioned, you need to take the time to write one before creating your community outreach plan. You may believe you cannot afford to take the time necessary to write or update a long-range plan. In reality, having a plan in place will save you time, money, and manpower. Perhaps you feel you lack the knowledge to write a plan. If so, use the information provided in this section of the manual along with the worksheets for Chapter 2 to help you write a succinct yet meaningful long-range plan.

Let's take a look at the components of a basic long-range plan, the vision and mission statements, goals and objectives, and activities and action plans. As we do, keep in mind how potential community outreach projects would support and enhance your library's vision and mission.

Vision Statement

Definition: A vision statement is a sentence or short paragraph that provides a broad image of the future the library seeks to create. It is what the library aspires to become.

The vision statement describes why it is important for the library to achieve its mission. It defines the purpose or broader goal for the library's existence. It serves as your inspiration and provides the framework for planning. It answers the question, "Where do we want to go?" You are articulating your dreams and hopes for your library when you write the library's vision statement. The vision statement provides a constant reminder of what kind of library you are trying to develop.

The vision you have for your library is the first step in determining the direction you will take in the materials and services you provide for your community. Vision statements are as varied as the communities that libraries serve. A good vision statement provides in one or two succinct sentences what broad overall role you would like the library to play in your community. It identifies the future you are striving to create.

These are some common roles of public libraries:

- Lifelong learning
- Community commons
- Heritage center
- Gateway to information
- Current topics and titles
- Formal education support

Examples of vision statements include the following:

- The library improves lives by providing information to all citizens to meet their cultural, recreational, and educational needs.
- The library is the center of lifelong learning for all residents.
- The library serves as the information center for the city and surrounding communities.
- The library is the community's gathering place and center for educational and recreational information.
- The library is the building block for the future development of the city and its citizens.
- The library is the information hub of the community.
- The library provides opportunities for cultural, personal, and intellectual enrichment in a safe and welcoming environment.
- The library serves people of different cultures and ages using best practices to improve the quality of life and provide educational opportunities for all.
- The library acts as a bridge between citizens and knowledge and as the community's gathering place.
- The library provides access to innovative library services to meet the informational, educational, recreational, and technological needs of the diverse populations it serves.

Mission Statement

Definition: A mission statement is the library's reason for being and should reflect the library's core purpose, identity, values, and primary focus.

The mission statement defines the fundamental purpose of an organization and succinctly describes why it exists and what it does to achieve the library's vision. The mission statement is more specific than the vision statement and provides a path to realize the vision in line with the library's values. It should be a short one- to two-sentence summary of the purpose of the library.

The mission statement answers the questions, "Who are we, and what do we do?" It articulates the library's purpose both for those within the organization and for the public. It should reflect the values of the community and the qualities that make the library unique.

Services commonly provided by a public library include customer service; information and/or reference assistance; current educational and recreational materials; programs; literacy; Internet access and computers; and meeting rooms for public use. Core values held by many libraries include excellent customer service; professional ethics; intellectual freedom; free and open access to recorded knowledge, information, and creative works; commitment to literacy and learning; respect for the diversity of all people; preservation of local history; collaboration and partnership; and friendly and welcoming environment.

These are good examples of mission statements:

- The mission of the library is to provide citizens of all ages with a high-quality facility and services consistent with available community resources.
- The mission of the library is to provide library services delivered in an efficient and effective manner to enable library users to grow and learn throughout their lives, to find and use information in a variety of formats, and to explore their personal heritage.
- The mission of the library is to provide excellent customer service and reference assistance; give patrons of all ages, all economic backgrounds, and all cultural diversities the means for lifelong learning; and meet the educational and recreational needs of the community by providing high-quality materials in a variety of formats.
- The mission of the library is to provide recreational, informational, and educational services to all adults and juveniles in the city and county; to make current information available in a wide variety of formats; to offer materials to enhance lifelong learning, and to develop broad community awareness of the library and its services.
- The mission of the library is to give people of all ages a means to continue to learn throughout their lives and to meet their educational and recreational reading needs through a variety of materials and programs.
- The mission of the library is to provide an environment that fulfills the need of its patrons to meet and interact with others in the community and to participate in educational and recreational programs on a variety of subjects.

- The mission of the library is to be a leader in the community by providing friendly and professional service along with a diverse collection of materials and online resources to address the informational, educational, and recreational needs of all members of the community.

IN & OUT: Program Ideas

Target Groups: Parents, Children, Teens

Program Types:

1. Teen Summer Reading Program
2. Family Health Fair
3. Parenting Skills for Pregnant Teens

Potential Partners:

Local schools, boys and girls clubs, teen church groups, Vacation Bible School programs, homeschool associations, family service agencies, health care centers, and hospitals are possible partners for family or age-specific health programs.

Resources:

KidsHealth is one of the largest resources online for medically reviewed health information written for parents, kids, and teens. It can be found at http://kidshealth.org. The website states:

> Created by the Nemours Center for Children's Health Media, KidsHealth has a physician-directed, professional editorial staff expert at making these often complex and sensitive medical topics understandable. Since 1995, KidsHealth has been the #1 most-visited, most-recognized online source of information about children's health and development. Most of KidsHealth's funding comes from Nemours, one of the nation's largest nonprofits dedicated to children's health care, research, advocacy, and education.

There are separate sections of the website for parents, kids, and teens. The information on this website in each section (parents, kids, teens) lends itself to the development of a myriad of programs. Libraries could have a variety of programs to bring awareness to the website or could have a number of specific programs dealing with one of the topics covered. There are also resources such as school lesson plans and brochures that could be used as is or modified for an outreach program. The media permissions guideline (found at http://kidshealth.org/media/permissions/) states: "KidsHealth allows articles to be printed and used as handouts, provided they are distributed at no charge to the recipients. There is no limit to the number of copies that can be printed; use the 'printer-friendly' version, which can be accessed from a link at the bottom of each article."

IN the Library:

1. **Teen Summer Reading Program**: Hold a scavenger-type contest using the TeensHealth part of the website as the basis for the program. Have a list of information the teens must find with prizes for the winners. The topics on TeensHealth include your body; your mind; sexual health; food and fitness; recipes; drugs and alcohol; expert answers; diseases and conditions; infections; school and jobs; and staying safe.
2. **Family Health Fair**: Partner with the local health agency or migrant teen office to have a family health fair at the library for Spanish-speaking parents and their children (teens and kids). The library teaches the families about the KidsHealth website and how to use it. Workstations with appropriate activities are set up for parents, kids, and teens. Volunteers from the library's partner groups man the workstations and do demonstrations of the information available suitable for that particular age group. Food, prizes, and games are included as part of the program.

OUT of the Library:

1. **Parenting Skills for Pregnant Teens**: Partner with the local high school to provide parenting skills to pregnant teens. Do a presentation about the website to the class. Teach the students how to find the information they want and need by covering the resources and topics on the website. Topics covered include general health; infections; emotions and behavior; growth and development; nutrition and fitness; recipes; pregnancy and newborns; medical problems; positive parenting; first aid and safety; doctors and hospitals; and medications. The information is also provided in Español.

- The mission of the library is to provide materials in a variety of formats and programs to give citizens the means to continue to learn throughout life; to find, evaluate, and use information; to pursue formal and personal educational goals; to gain knowledge; and to fulfill their recreational and social reading interests as individuals and as a family.
- The mission of the library is to provide access to library services delivered in an efficient and effective manner and to provide materials, information, and programs to meet the educational and recreational needs of the community.
- The mission of the library is to provide informational and educational services to all adults and juveniles in the city; to provide the most wanted materials as defined by public demand in both print and nonprint within budgetary constraints; to develop broad community awareness of the library and its services; and to supplement but not necessarily duplicate the materials and/or services of other local libraries.
- The mission of the library is to provide its patrons, regardless of age or nationality, the resources, materials, and programs to meet their needs; to provide the information services needed to answer their questions; and to promote and establish a love of reading and learning, especially in children.
- It is the mission of the library to enable everyone to achieve their full potential by empowering them with information and knowledge. The library strives to select, organize, preserve, and make available materials in a variety of formats to meet the recreational, educational, cultural, and informational needs of the diverse community it serves.
- The mission of the library is to provide free and open access to recreational and educational information; promote informational freedom; promote a love and respect of the written word; respect the individuality and diversity of all people; and provide efficient and quality service to all library users.

Goals

Definition: A goal is the result or achievement toward which effort is directed. Goals focus on ends rather than means and describe future outcomes or states. They have observable and measurable end results with one or more objectives to be achieved within a specified timeframe. Goals should be tied to the focus and services the library provides as identified in the library's vision and mission statements. The question, "Has the goal been achieved?" can always be answered with either a yes or a no.

When setting goals, first you must decide what it is that you want to accomplish. Then devise a plan to achieve the results you desire. Goals without action plans are like plans without a deadline, just dreams. Make sure the goals you set are specific, measurable and attainable, time bound, and meaningful. If a goal isn't meaningful to the people tasked with accomplishing it, there will not be enough motivation to see it through to completion.

These are examples of specific, meaningful goals:

- Promote a lifelong love of reading.
- Maintain a current, quality collection of educational and recreational materials.
- Develop community partnerships.
- Be a gathering place for the community.

Objectives

Definition: Objectives are specific, clearly defined, realistic, measurable, and time-limited statements of actions that when completed will move the library toward achieving its stated goal. Objectives answer the question, "How can we accomplish the goal?"

Examples of effective objectives include the following:

- For the goal "Promote a lifelong love of reading," one objective is, "Help develop early reading skills."
- For the goal "Promote a lifelong love of reading," one objective is, "Help maintain and/or improve children's reading skills."

Objectives can be broken down into activities to be done and the tasks necessary to do the activity.

Activities

Definition: An activity is a unit of work associated with accomplishing an objective. An activity has a definite duration, is related to the other activities associated with accomplishing the objective, includes the defined resources needed to accomplish the activity, and includes the associated cost in time, money, manpower, and resources. Activities are the building blocks of an action plan. Activities answer the question, "What are the steps necessary to accomplish the objective?"

Tasks

Definition: Tasks are the step-by-step actions taken to accomplish the stated activity. Tasks are the smallest unit of work in the action plan.

Action Plan

Definition: An action plan includes goals, objectives, and activities with the actions, people, resources, time, and funding needed for each activity involved in meeting the objective and achieving the goal. It includes how you will monitor and evaluate the effort expended.

Creating an action plan is a step frequently overlooked during planning. In strategic planning the primary focus is often on writing the vision,

IN & OUT: Program Ideas

Target Groups: Children, Teens, Adults, and Seniors

Program Types:

1. After-School Read with a Dog
2. Summer Reading Program Dog Days
3. Raise Awareness of Therapy Dogs
4. Facilitate Use of Therapy Dogs with Homebound

Potential Partners:

Assisted living centers, nursing homes, schools, hospitals, hospice care, civic organizations, and local media outlets are all potential partners.

Resources:

Therapy Dogs International (TDI) is a nonprofit volunteer organization founded in 1976 dedicated to the regulation, testing, and registration of therapy dogs and their volunteer handlers. It maintains a registry of volunteer dogs and handlers for all 50 states. The website address is http://tdi-dog.org/Default.aspx. The website provides information on programs featuring therapy dogs, including Tail Waggin' Tutors; Disaster Stress Relief Dog Program; Assisted Living; Home Visits; Hospice; Hospitals (Children's); Hospitals (General); Libraries; Nursing Homes; Schools; Shelters; and the Final Visit (funerals).

IN the Library:

1. **After-School Read with a Dog**: Contact TDI to set up a Tail Waggin' Tutors program in the library. As TDI explains on its website, the "Tail Waggin' Tutors" program encourages children to read by providing a nonjudgmental listener and furry friend to read to that won't laugh at them if they make a mistake or stumble over a word but rather lie next to them and enjoy the story being read to them. The children learn to associate reading with being with the dog and begin to view reading in a positive way. Over time, children's reading ability and confidence can improve because they are practicing their skills, which will make them enjoy reading even more. Libraries have had great success by utilizing "Tail Waggin' Tutors" as part of their Summer Reading Program or After-School Program.
2. **Summer Reading Program Dog Days**: Have one or more therapy dogs available for children to read to one day each week of the Summer Reading Program.
3. **Raise Awareness of Therapy Dogs**: Host a TDI presentation. Ask a therapy dog handler to do a presentation on the programs available geared toward nursing homes, assisted living centers, schools, funeral homes, homebound, and during disaster recovery. Invite civic organizations, fire and police department representatives (disaster recovery), Red Cross, church leaders, activity directors for assisted living centers and nursing homes, hospice care, and school representatives to attend. Have informational brochures and other relevant handouts along with refreshments.

OUT of the Library:

1. **Raise Awareness of Therapy Dogs**: Partner with a local veterinarian to have a program on therapy dogs at his or her facility for potential therapy dog handlers. Facilitate the program by contacting the potential speaker, procuring brochures and other handouts, and publicizing and promoting the program. The same type of program can also be held in conjunction with a local pet shop.
2. **Facilitate Use of Therapy Dogs with Homebound**: If the library has a homebound service, consider working with other agencies or organizations to have a therapy dog visit the homebound. The library could survey the people taking part in the homebound reading program to see if they would like to have a therapy dog visit. This information could be provided to the organization wishing to arrange for the dogs to visit the homebound.

mission, goals, and objectives. The action plan may be perceived as being too daunting because of the level of detail involved or as not being as necessary as the planning that has already taken place. Because of that, it may be set aside to be done at a later date, but somehow the day never comes to sit down and write the action plan.

The action plan is critical to success. It lays out the plan of attack, the nitty-gritty, nuts and bolts in terms of time, people, and resources needed to accomplish each goal and objective. The action plan pulls it all together, providing a clear picture of where you are going, how you will get there, who and what are involved to get there, the timeframe, and a method to monitor your progress and assess your success.

Keep in mind that the action plan is a guide, not a set of rules and regulations. It may be necessary to adjust one or more components of the action plan after it has been written due to a change in personnel or funding.

To write or revise your library vision and mission statements, goals and objectives, or action plans, see Worksheets 2.1 through 2.4 (pp. 13–17). They are designed to guide you through the process.

Community Profile

Next let's look at your community and your library's place in it. It can be helpful to learn about or review the geographic, demographic, and statistical characteristics of your service area along with the role the library has historically and currently plays in it. This can help you identify factors that impact service needs and delivery, potential underserved groups, and additional roles the library could play in the future through your outreach plan.

The first step is to identify or define the community that you want to work with. For a small or rural library, the community will probably be the entire town and perhaps the rural area in which it is situated. For large urban libraries, the community in question may be the entire metropolis, or it may be a defined segment or subset. It may be a single neighborhood served by a specific branch, or it may be some other well-defined segment of the larger community. Regardless of the size and setting of your library, the key in developing an effective outreach plan is to first identify and define the community that you propose to serve.

Factors of Geography

Where geographically is your town, county, or service area located, and how does its location influence the character of the community? For example, if your community is located far from other towns or cities and the primary industry is farming, what are the main crops that are farmed? Are they ones that employ migrant workers? If so, you may have a large migrant population that may be an underserved population that would benefit from a library outreach program.

Is your community located geographically close to much larger towns with more economic opportunities? If so, you may have a bedroom community with a large portion of the population that drives to another town daily to work. This could be an underserved population that you could reach through special programs and targeted promotion. Conversely, if your community is one that attracts a large number of commuters, you might target them as an underserved segment of your daytime

(Continued p. 18)

WORKSHEET 2.1. VISION STATEMENT

A good vision statement is a sentence or a short paragraph consisting of two to four sentences. To help you write or revise the vision statement for your library, complete the exercise below. Take your time, and use the examples provided in the "Vision Statement" chapter section to get a feel for a completed vision statement.

List two to three defining aspects of your community, such as "ranching, farming, and oil industry."

List two to three defining aspects of your library, such as "shared facility with city hall."

List the current role(s) the library fulfills in the community, such as a "gathering place."

List what role(s) you would like the library to fulfill, such as "lifelong learning center."

List the services the library currently provides, such as "Internet access."

List any additional services you would like the library to provide, such as "Wi-Fi hotspot."

List the groups of people who currently use the library, such as "children, mothers, and retired."

List any groups of people who do not currently use the library whom you want to attract, such as "migrant families and teens."

List the impact you would like the library to have on the community and its residents, such as "improve the quality of life" or "create lifelong learners."

List some positive words of aspiration and inspiration to describe your library, its services, and the community you serve, such as "excellent, friendly, and professional."

Identify the most important points and your keywords. Combine them into one or two sentences. Make your vision statement positive and inspirational.

Draft Vision Statement:

Final Vision Statement:

WORKSHEET 2.2. MISSION STATEMENT
The mission statement defines the purpose of the library in one or two sentences. To help you write or review the mission statement for your library, complete the exercise below. Take your time, and use the examples of mission statements provided in the "Mission Statement" chapter section to help you write a short, to-the-point mission statement that articulates what the library does, how it does it, and why it does it.
List the services and functions of your library.
List the core values of the library, such as "friendly staff and quality materials."
List why you do what you do, such as "to develop lifelong learners" or "to promote a love of reading."
Look at the list you made of services and functions, and identify the primary purpose of the library.
Add how you fulfill the primary purpose, such as "provide educational and recreational materials in a variety of formats."
Add the core value associated with the primary purpose.
Add why you do what you do to describe the impact the library wants to have.
Identify the secondary purpose of the library, and describe it.
Add how you fulfill the secondary purpose.
Add the core value associated with the purpose.
Add why you do what you do to describe the impact of the secondary purpose.
Combine the identified purposes into one or two sentences. For example, "The mission of the library is to provide a high-quality collection of educational and recreational materials in a variety of formats to promote the development of lifelong learners." **Draft Mission Statement:** **Final Mission Statement:**

WORKSHEET 2.3. GOALS AND OBJECTIVES

The goal should focus on the benefit your library users or specific group will receive as a result of the goal being accomplished. Goals should be stated before objectives, are general in nature, and are important on their own. They are best when written in terms of major responsibilities, services provided, areas of need, or programs.

GOALS

Area of Responsibility the Goal Addresses	Library Service to Which It Relates	Area of Need It Addresses

State the Goals:

At least one objective should be written for each goal. The objective specifies how you will accomplish the goal. Objectives are more than just activities; they should contain some challenge in them. If an objective does nothing toward achieving the goal it relates to, then change or replace the objective, and add one that does further the goal. Remember, activities are step-by-step tasks you do to accomplish the objective; they are not the objective itself.

OBJECTIVES FOR GOAL 1

Objective to Accomplish to Meet the Goal	Date to Be Completed

State the Objective(s):

(Continued)

WORKSHEET 2.3. GOALS AND OBJECTIVES *(Continued)*

OBJECTIVES FOR GOAL 2

Objective to Accomplish to Meet the Goal	Date to Be Completed

State the Objective(s):

OBJECTIVES FOR GOAL 3

Objective to Accomplish to Meet the Goal	Date to Be Completed

State the Objective(s):

OBJECTIVES FOR GOAL 4

Objective to Accomplish to Meet the Goal	Date to Be Completed

State the Objective(s):

WORKSHEET 2.4. ACTION PLAN

Write the first goal and its objectives.

Goal:

Objectives:

Create an action plan for each objective. In the table, record the actions and resources you will use to achieve the objectives for the goal. Record how you will measure and evaluate the results. Copy this worksheet and use one form for each objective if you have more than one for the goal. Repeat the process for each goal.

ACTION PLAN GRID

IMPLEMENTATION			EVALUATION	
Action What action, activity, or task needs to be done?	**Name and Date** Who will do it, and by what date will it be done?	**Resources Needed** How much time, money, materials, and personnel are needed?	**Measurement** How will progress be measured (#, % of participation or attendance)?	**Analysis** How and when will data be gathered and analyzed to determine success?

population. If your community is a large urban area, you will find different demographic, economic, and social factors are dominant.

A second dimension to consider related to geography is the physical location of the library building. Is it a stand-alone facility or a shared-use space? If it is a stand-alone building, where in the community is it in relation to other organizations and agencies? Is it near a school, hospital, city hall, parks and recreation, animal shelter, churches, or businesses? If it is a shared-use space, with what other agency or organization does the library share? In a large urban system, you will need to determine whether the frame of reference for your plan is systemwide, involving all of the facilities, or some other subset, down to a single branch.

Take some time to flesh out a geographic picture of your library and the community it seeks to serve. Get a good map, take a drive around the community, and photograph relevant features to begin developing a visual picture of your service area. Add these to your planning documents. They can be used later if you wish when doing presentations to potential sponsors or to those you approach for funding for the outreach you want to do to reach a particular underserved group. To help you develop your geographic picture of your community, use Worksheet 2.5.

WORKSHEET 2.5. COMMUNITY GEOGRAPHICS

Use this worksheet to identify geographic features of your community and the geographic relationship of your library to other buildings in the community.

GEOGRAPHIC—COMMUNITY FEATURES

For those you believe are an asset to your community, place an "A" before the feature. For those you feel create a challenge for the community, place a "C" before the feature.

Mountains	Hills
Sand Dunes	Farmland
Rivers	Valley
Desert	Forest
Ponds	Lake
Public Swimming Pool	Public Parks
Tennis Courts	Soccer Fields
Water Park	Oil Fields
Cattle Ranches	Horse Ranches
Fairgrounds	Rodeo Grounds
Exotic Animal Ranches	Bird Sanctuary
Railroad Lines	Municipal Golf Course
Tree Farm/Orchards	Corn Maze
Vineyard	Observatory
Military Base	Historical Site
Hot Springs	Natural Springs
Archaeological Site	Historic Fort

(Continued)

WORKSHEET 2.5. COMMUNITY GEOGRAPHICS *(Continued)*

GEOGRAPHIC—COMMUNITY FEATURES *(Continued)*	*(Place an "A" for asset or a "C" for challenge before the feature.)*
Miles to Nearest Town	Major Highways
Miles to Larger City	Miles to Major City
Pumpkin Patch	Bridges
Dams	Reservoir
Mine	Bayous
Levee	Quarry
Fish Farms	Dairy Farms
Electrical Power Plant	Wind Turbines
Nuclear Power Plant	Caves
Semiprecious Stones	Seed Farms
Precious Metals/Minerals	Chicken Farm
Public Land	Fish and Game Land Leases
Waterways	Fishing Industry
Water Land/Marshland	Migratory Path
Airport	Harbor
Hiking Trails	Walking Trails
Biking Trails	Campgrounds

GEOGRAPHIC—LIBRARY RELATIONSHIPS

Use an "A" for those you consider to be an asset to providing services or programs. Use a "C" for those you feel create a challenge for the library. Use an "N" for those near the library.

Stand-Alone Facility	Shared Facility with (Insert Name)
Elementary School	Church, Synagogue, Mosque
High School	Middle School
Community College	Vo-Tech School
City Hall	University
Chamber of Commerce	County Courthouse
Hospital	Health Clinic
Rehabilitation Center	Health Department
Country Club	Mental Health Center
Day Care	Halfway House
Family Crisis Center	Local Workforce Office
Senior Citizens Center	Youth Center
American Legion	Bingo Hall
Casino	Tribal Center
Department of Protective Services	Orphanage
Youth Home	Homeless Shelter
Food Bank	Thrift Shop
Newspaper Office	Cable/Satellite TV

(Continued)

WORKSHEET 2.5. COMMUNITY GEOGRAPHICS *(Continued)*

GEOGRAPHIC—LIBRARY RELATIONSHIPS *(Continued)* *(Use "A" for asset, "C" for challenge, or "N" for those near library.)*

Utilities (Electric, Water)	Telephone Office
Post Office	Domestic Violence Center
Adult Care Center	Nursing Home
Assisted Living Center	Theater
Community Center	Bowling Alley
Fire Station	Skating Rink
Police Station	Correctional Facility/Jail
RV Park	Sheriff's Office
Railroad Depot	Juvenile Detention Center
Bus Station	Department of Transportation
Department of Public Safety	Civic Center
Public Housing	Animal Shelter
Golf Club	Spa/Health Club
Resort	County Extension Office
Grocery Store	Historical Building
Museum	Art Gallery
Visitor Center	Performing Arts Center
Tourism Center	Historical Commission
Arts Commission	Art Studio
Dance Studio	Retail Shop
Martial Arts Studio	Exercise or Fitness Center
School for the Blind	School for the Deaf
Print/Photocopy Shop	Tennis Club
Hospice Center	Border Patrol
Apartments	Animal Hospital/Vet
Bookstore	Coffee Shop
Bakery/Doughnut Shop	Fast Food Restaurant
Fine Dining Restaurant	Ice Cream Shop
Family Restaurant	Truck Stop

List the prominent geographic features found in your community and the buildings/facilities in close proximity to your library.

Main Geographic Features:

Community Features:

Assets and Challenges:

Main Buildings Close to the Library:

Library Features:

Assets and Challenges:

Demographic and Statistical Data

The U.S. Census Bureau at http://www.census.gov/ has the most extensive website for current census demographic and statistical data. It is especially good for income, poverty, and population projection information. American Fact Finder at http://factfinder.census.gov/ has easy-to-search data arranged both alphabetically and geographically. It includes information on population, housing, economics, and geography. FEDStats at http://www.fedstats.gov provides links to more than 100 agencies along with a description of the statistics accessible through each agency's websites. A good source for state and county demographic data is the U.S. Census Bureau's State and County QuickFacts website at http://quickfacts.census.gov/qfd/index.html.

Figure 2.1 (pp. 22–23) illustrates the use of the U.S. Census Bureau's State and County QuickFacts website to compile demographic information about Andrews County, Texas (from http://quickfacts.census.gov/qfd/states/). Note the types of demographic information provided related to population, age, race, housing, income, and languages that you can access about your county. For this example, you would:

(Continued p. 24)

IN & OUT: Program Ideas

Target Group: Senior Citizens

Program Type: CLIC-on-Health for Seniors Training Program

Potential Partners:

The local senior citizens center, local health agencies, health clinics, hospitals, doctors, assisted living centers, retirement centers, and nursing homes are potential partners. Community radio, television, and newspaper outlets are possible partners for publicizing the program.

Resources:

CLIC-on-Health was created by the Rochester Regional Library Council (RRLC) in New York. RRLC brought together medical, public, and school librarians, along with local health agency representatives, to create and implement a program that would make Rochester a healthier community. The website has a multitude of resources. The address is http://www.cliconhealth.org.

One resource is the CLIC-on-Health for Seniors program developed through a partnership of libraries and senior centers to provide older adults in the Rochester, New York, region easy access to consumer health information on the Internet. The senior citizens centers and living facilities that participated in the project were located in urban, suburban, and rural settings. This model, funded by a grant from the National Institutes of Health, National Library of Medicine, can be repeated or modified for any location offering services to older adults using the manuals they created. The manuals, one for libraries and one for senior centers, provide information on how to set up or continue a training program for seniors about using the computer and Internet to find trustworthy online sources of medical information.

IN the Library:

Use the *CLIC-on-Health for Seniors Training Program: Manual for Libraries* found on WebJunction at http://www.webjunction.org/470/articles/content/455042 as a model to develop your own in-library program.

OUT of the Library:

Provide your local senior citizens center a copy of the *CLIC-on-Health for Seniors Training Program: Manual for Senior Centers* found on WebJunction at http://www.webjunction.org/470/articles/content/455033. Use this as a way to facilitate a joint project between the library and center to provide training for seniors.

Figure 2.1. Demographic Data for Andrews County, Texas

Andrews County, Texas	Want more? Browse data sets for Andrews County	
People QuickFacts	**Andrews County**	**Texas**
Population, 2009 estimate	14,057	24,782,302
Population, percent change, April 1, 2000 to July 1, 2009	8.1%	18.8%
Population estimates base (April 1) 2000	13,004	20,851,818
Persons under 5 years old, percent, 2009	8.8%	8.4%
Persons under 18 years old, percent, 2009	30.5%	27.8%
Persons 65 years old and over, percent, 2009	11.3%	10.2%
Female persons, percent, 2009	50.2%	50.1%
White persons, percent, 2009 (a)	94.3%	82.1%
Black persons, percent, 2009 (a)	2.6%	12.0%
American Indian and Alaska Native persons, percent, 2009 (a)	1.1%	0.8%
Asian persons, percent, 2009 (a)	0.9%	3.6%
Native Hawaiian and Other Pacific Islander, percent, 2009 (a)	Z	0.1%
Persons reporting two or more races, percent, 2009	0.9%	1.4%
Persons of Hispanic or Latino origin, percent, 2009 (b)	49.1%	36.9%
White persons not Hispanic, percent, 2009	46.5%	46.7%
Living in same house in 1995 and 2000, pct 5 yrs old & over	63.3%	49.6%
Foreign-born persons, percent, 2000	10.6%	13.9%
Language other than English spoken at home, pct age 5+, 2000	33.6%	31.2%
High school graduates, percent of persons age 25+, 2000	68.0%	75.7%
Bachelor's degree or higher, pct of persons age 25+, 2000	12.4%	23.2%
Persons with a disability, age 5+, 2000	2,154	3,605,542
Mean travel time to work (minutes), workers age 16+, 2000	20.6	25.4
Housing units, 2009	5,810	9,724,251
Homeownership rate, 2000	79.7%	63.8%
Housing units in multi-unit structures, percent, 2000	6.7%	24.2%
Median value of owner-occupied housing units, 2000	$42,500	$82,500
Households, 2000	4,601	7,393,354

(Continued)

Figure 2.1. Demographic Data for Andrews County, Texas *(Continued)*

Andrews County, Texas	Want more? Browse data sets for Andrews County	
People QuickFacts *(Continued)*	**Andrews County**	**Texas**
Persons per household, 2000	2.81	2.74
Median household income, 2008	$49,043	$50,049
Per capita money income, 1999	$15,916	$19,617
Persons below poverty level, percent, 2008	13.4%	15.8%
Business QuickFacts	**Andrews County**	**Texas**
Private nonfarm establishments, 2007	311	521,408[1]
Private nonfarm employment, 2007	4,081	9,041,030[1]
Private nonfarm employment, percent change 2000–2007	45.3%	12.6%[1]
Nonemployer establishments, 2007	958	1,819,963
Total number of firms, 2002	1,018	1,734,509
Black-owned firms, percent, 2002	F	5.1%
American Indian- and Alaska Native-owned firms, percent, 2002	F	0.9%
Asian-owned firms, percent, 2002	F	4.5%
Native Hawaiian- and Other Pacific Islander-owned firms, percent, 2002	F	0.1%
Hispanic-owned firms, percent, 2002	F	18.4%
Women-owned firms, percent, 2002	28.3%	27.0%
Manufacturers' shipments, 2002 ($1000)	NA	310,815,965
Wholesale trade sales, 2002 ($1000)	D	397,405,111
Retail sales, 2002 ($1000)	65,380	228,694,755
Retail sales per capita, 2002	$5,059	$10,528
Accommodation and foodservices sales, 2002 ($1000)	7,221	29,914,774
Building permits, 2009	46	84,440
Federal spending, 2008	93,510	210,004,633[1]
Geography QuickFacts	**Andrews County**	**Texas**
Land area, 2000 (square miles)	1,500.64	261,797.12
Persons per square mile, 2000	8.7	79.6
FIPS Code	003	48
Metropolitan or Micropolitan Statistical Area	Andrews, TX Micro Area	

1. Go to http://quickfacts.census.gov/qfd/states/.
2. Select Texas from the dropdown box provided.
3. Select Andrews County from the dropdown box provided.

Again, the purpose of looking at the data is to get a clearer picture of the makeup of your community and to ascertain factors that can help you identify underserved or special needs segments of your population. It is also useful when writing grant requests or requests for funding to foundations, businesses, or private trusts.

Library Profile

Developing a library profile before writing your outreach plan will help you identify what you are already doing and what resources are committed. This will help you determine if you have the time, manpower, funding, and resources to do the outreach program or project you have in mind.

It will also give you an opportunity to decide if there are existing programs or projects that no longer serve a useful purpose. Perhaps at one time a particular program was needed, wanted, and well attended, but now the need no longer exists, it is no longer attended, or its timeliness has passed. If that is the case, discontinue the program and free up those resources to use for your new programs or projects.

Sometimes people continue doing a program long past its time. The reasons for this vary. It may be political. For example, the program is the pet program of the mayor, chair of the library board, or the Friends of the Library. It might be staff based. For example, the children's librarian has done a special witches and warlocks program during the summer reading program for the past 10 years even though now there is on the average only 3 to 4 children attending the program when in the past there was an average of 20 to 30 attendees. Or it might be your personal pet project. Regardless of why it has been allowed to continue past its time, cut it. Why? Because that tired program is eating away time, money, manpower, and physical resources that could be better used in a new, exciting, and needed program. Programs, like books, need to be weeded. Use Worksheet 2.6 to help you review your existing programs.

You can access statistical data from various reports you prepare for your governing entity or library board. In addition, if you complete an annual report for your state library you will have access to that information. For example, the Texas State Library and Archives Commission makes this information accessible on its website. Librarians can go to the Texas Public Library Statistics section of the website (http://www.tsl.state.tx.us/ld/pubs/pls/2009/index.html) and access an easy-to-use search feature to pull up annual report data for most public libraries in the state. The data for the library includes usage statistics, among other things. Figure 2.2 (p. 26) shows the Texas Public Library's statistics search options.

Figure 2.3 (p. 27) shows the kind of information that can be found for a library, in this case the Andrews County (Texas) Library. For this example, you would:

WORKSHEET 2.6. EXISTING PROGRAMS

Put K (Keep), C (Cut), or M (Marginal) by all the ones your library offers.

Regular Lap Sit Program	Regular Toddler Storytime
Regular Storytime for Preschool	Regular Storytime for Day Care Centers
Summer Reading Program for Children	Summer Reading Program for Teens
Winter Reading Program for Children	Canned Food Drive
Adult Book Club	Adult Reading Program
Family Literacy Program	Teen Book Club
Work Skills Assistance (classes/programs)	Regular Family Film/Fun Night
Spanish Language Classes	Homeschool Programs
Regular Computer Gaming Programs	English Language Classes
Basic Computer Literacy Classes	Regular Gaming Programs
Nursing Home Outreach	Assisted Living Center Outreach
Homebound Outreach	Migrant Outreach
Outreach to Homeless	Regular Author Visits
Regular Lecture Series	English as a Second Language Program
GED Preparation Tutoring	Exam Proctoring
Literacy Program with Tutors and Students	Interlibrary Loan
Preparation for Citizenship Classes	Storytime in Spanish
Teen Blog (maintained by library staff)	Scrapbooking with Library Dies
Library Wiki (maintained by library staff)	Memory Books for Teens
Regular Art Displays	Regular Genealogy Programs
Project to Create Local Photo Archive	Digitalizing Local History Project
Digitalizing Local History Photo Archive	Digitalizing Local Newspaper
Digitalizing Local Government Records	Digitalizing Local Cemetery Gravestones
Digitalizing Local Church Historical Records	Digitalizing Local Funeral Home Records
Digitalizing Local Cemetery Records	Digitalizing Local Obituaries

List the ones to cut and the ones that are marginal which you need to either revamp or cut later.

Programs to Cut:

Marginal Programs to Revamp or Cut Later:

Figure 2.2. Search Options for Statistics on the Texas Public Library Website

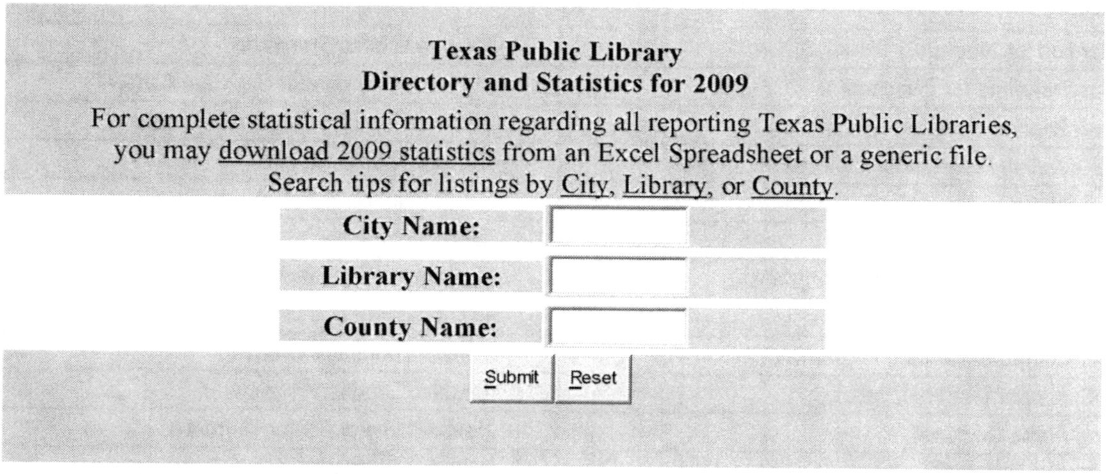

Texas Public Library
Directory and Statistics for 2009

For complete statistical information regarding all reporting Texas Public Libraries, you may download 2009 statistics from an Excel Spreadsheet or a generic file.
Search tips for listings by City, Library, or County.

City Name:

Library Name:

County Name:

Submit Reset

1. Go to http://www.tsl.state.tx.us/ld/pubs/pls/2009/index.html.
2. Enter Andrews in the City Name search box.
3. Click the Submit button.
4. For Andrews, it will take you to the following address: http://www.tsl.state.tx.us/ld/pubs/pls/2009/plsresults.php.
5. Click the Display Statistics button.
6. This will take you to http://www.tsl.state.tx.us/ld/pubs/pls/2009/plsstats.php where you will find the information in Figure 2.3.

It is useful to have this data because different pieces of information will become relevant as you create your outreach plan. The data you need will depend on the particular outreach program or project you are striving to implement. Use Worksheet 2.7 (p. 28) to help you get a picture of the demographics of your community and library statistical data.

Library's Role in the Community

Examining the role of the library in the community is important. Look at the role the library has played historically and is playing currently, and think about what role you would like for it to play in the future. The reason this is useful to do before writing your outreach plan is because it brings to your awareness the perception people in your community have of the library in contrast to your vision of the library.

You can get input from others by giving the Library Roles Worksheet (2.8, p. 31) to:

- members of the library staff, board, and friends group;
- governing entities such as the city manager, county commissioners, or county judge;

Figure 2.3. Statistical Data about the Andrews County Library

Andrews County Library

GENERAL	
City	Andrews
System	WTLS
County	Andrews
Legal Establishment	County
Membership status (SFY 2011)	M
Population served	13,645
Number of branches	0
Number of bookmobiles	0
EXPENDITURES ($)	
Salaries and wages	309,506
Employee benefits	136,282
Subtotal: wages and benefits	445,788
Print materials including serials in print	50,735
Electronic materials	450
Other materials	14,753
Subtotal: library materials	65,938
Other operating expenses	57,600
Total direct expenditures	569,326
Indirect costs	0
Total operating expenditures	569,326
Salaries wages per capita	22.68
Materials expenditures per capita	4.83
Total operating expenditures per capita	41.72
Capital outlay	0
Total local operating expenditures:	569,326
% of Total Operating Expenses	
• Wages benefits	78.30%
• Library materials	11.58%
• Miscellaneous other	10.12%
• Indirect costs	0.00%
INCOME BY SOURCE ($)	
City	0
County	556,792
School district	0
Subtotal: local government income	556,792
Foundation and corporate grants	0
Federal LSTA funds	0
Other federal funds	0
State funds	8,131
Other local income	12,534
Subtotal: all other income	12,534
Total income	577,457
Local government income per capita	40.81
Total income per capita	42.32

LIBRARY COLLECTION	
Books serials—titles	68,948
Books serials—items	74,884
Books serials—items per capita	5.49
Electronic books	0
Local licensed databases	2
Audio and Video Items	4,119
Total collection—titles	72,880
Total collections—items	79,005
Total collection—items per capita	5.79
Current subscriptions	83
LOCAL LIBRARY SERVICES	
Total library circulation	62,850
Circulation per capita	4.61
Circulation per paid staff member	7,856
Circulation per hour (overlapping)	22.70
Circulation per library visit	1.04
Number of registered borrowers	6,595
Circulation of juvenile materials	23,731
Collection turnover rate	0.80
Reference transactions	15,720
Reference transactions per capita	1.15
Library program attendance	6,142
Program attendance per capita	0.45
Attendance at juvenile programs	5,189
Number of terminals for Internet access	30
Number of library visits	60,206
Library visits per capita	4.41
Hours per week (non-overlapping)	58
STAFFING (FTEs)	
Librarians with ALA-MLS	0.00
Other librarians	4.00
Other paid staff	4.00
Total paid staff	8.00
Population per ALA-MLS	0
Population per total paid staff	1,706
Head librarian's salary ($)	54,691
Head librarian—hours per week	40
Total volunteer hours	513
FACILITIES	
Main library—square footage	19,990
Main + branch—square footage	19,990
Square footage per capita	1.47

WORKSHEET 2.7. DEMOGRAPHICS AND STATISTICS

Use this worksheet to identify important demographic and statistical data relevant to your library.

COMMUNITY DEMOGRAPHICS

Fill in the numbers. Put an "A" in front of those you consider to be an asset. Put a "C" in front of those you consider a challenge.

County	City
Population	Population
% under age 5	% under age 5
% under age 18	% under age 18
% over age 65	% over age 65
White Persons	White Persons
Black Persons	Black Persons
American Indian Persons	American Indian Persons
Asian Persons	Asian Persons
Hispanic or Latino Persons	Hispanic or Latino Persons
Foreign Born	Foreign Born
Language other than English	Language other than English
High School Graduate	High School Graduate
Bachelor's Degree	Bachelor's Degree
Median Drive Time to Work	Median Drive Time to Work
Persons with Disability	Persons with Disability
Housing Units	Housing Units
Households	Households
Median Household Income	Median Household Income

LIBRARY STATISTICS

Fill in the numbers. Put an "A" in front of those you consider to be an asset. Put a "C" before those you consider a challenge.

Population Served	# Programs
# of Registered Borrowers	# Program Attendance
# of Adults Registered	# Reference Transactions
# Teens Registered	# Interlibrary Loans
# of Juveniles Registered	# Website Hits
# of Branches	# Library Visits
# of Bookmobiles	# Computer Uses
# of Staff	# Circulations
# of Population Per Staff	# Titles in Collection
# of Volunteers	# Electronic Books
# of Volunteer Hours	# Licensed Databases
# Items in Collection	Square Feet of Library

Most Important Community Demographic Data:

Most Important Library Statistical Data:

- governing members of various organizations such as the chamber of commerce board, school board, or hospital board;
- other informal leaders such as graduates of the local leadership class (provided by many chamber of commerce organizations); prominent citizens from the major ethnic groups that make up your community; and student leaders from the local high school, vocational/technical school, or community college.

If you already have in mind potential group(s) you want to do an outreach program or project with, be sure to include a few members of those group(s) in your research. For example, if you are considering doing an outreach program for residents of a nursing home, give the worksheet to the administrator and the activities or program director (if it has one) as well as a couple of employees and residents of the nursing home that you are wanting to reach. This can provide valuable feedback to help you determine if the need exists and how to meet the need. It also serves as a way to engage the people you want to reach and as means to initiate meaningful dialog with the people you are trying to serve. By including them in the process in even a limited way you increase the likelihood of having a successful outreach project.

IN & OUT: Program Ideas

Target Groups: Blind, Disabled, Homebound, and Others in Long-Term Care

Program Types:

1. Develop Collection
2. Promote Awareness of Resources
3. Facilitate Access
4. Provide Materials to the Homebound

Potential Partners:

Local schools, churches, elder care facilities, hospices, senior citizens centers, health agencies, health clinics, hospitals, doctors, assisted living centers, retirement centers, civic organizations, and nursing homes are potential partners. In addition, community radio, television, and newspaper outlets are possible partners for publicizing the program.

Resources:

Libraries often purchase large-print books along with books on cassette or CD to provide a collection of materials for the vision impaired. While this is helpful, often there are individuals in the community who are unable to come to the library or who have limited ability to hold books or turn pages. The following resources can help you address these issues and extend your services to the target groups listed earlier.

1. Books Aloud, Inc., is a free service provider of audiobooks for people with special needs. According to the website (http://www.booksaloud.org/): "Books Aloud, Inc. is a 501(c)(3) non-profit organization supported by donations from individuals, corporations, foundations, trusts, businesses and service clubs and is a free service available nationwide." The company has 5,000+ unabridged titles that it lends out through its Reading by Listening program. Blind, visually impaired, learning disabled, or physically disabled individuals who are unable to read conventional print, hold a book, or turn pages are eligible. The website provides the application forms that must be completed. The website address is http://www.booksaloud.org/. An important feature of the books on tape provided through the Reading by Listening program is that users do not need special equipment to play the Books Aloud, Inc., tapes. They play on a standard cassette player.

(Continued)

IN & OUT: Program Ideas *(Continued)*

Resources *(Continued)*:

2. The National Library Service for the Blind and Physically Handicapped (NLS) Talking Books program is provided by the Library of Congress. The website address is http://www.loc.gov/nls/, where it states: "Talking Books is a free library service available to U.S. residents and citizens living abroad whose low vision, blindness, or physical handicap makes it difficult to read a standard printed page. Local cooperating libraries throughout the United States mail NLS audio books, magazines, and audio equipment directly to enrollees at no cost. Braille books and magazines are also available to patrons at no cost." The website provides the form borrowers must fill out along with the toll-free telephone number to call (1-888-NLS-READ). It also contains a searchable list of the national network of cooperating libraries through which NLS administers the free library program of Braille and audio materials circulated to eligible borrowers in the United States by postage-free mail. It is important to note that a special reader is required for the audiobooks available through this program. NLS does provide the special reader along with the audiobooks.

IN the Library:

1. **Develop Collection**: Purchase large-print books along with books on cassette or CD to provide a collection of materials for the vision impaired.
2. **Promote Awareness of Resources**: Create an audio description of the resources available for the vision impaired and others with special needs at the library and through organizations such as Books Aloud, Inc., and NLS. The library can also create informational handouts to distribute to schools, hospitals, churches, civic organizations, and appropriate facilities and agencies to get the word out.
3. **Facilitate Access**: Hold a workshop for local organizations that serve or work with the homebound, those in assisted living or nursing homes, and special needs individuals. At the workshop distribute the eligibility guidelines and copies of application forms for resources such as the Books Aloud, Inc., Reading by Listening, and the NLS Talking Book programs. Provide a tour of the materials (large-print book collection, books on tape, books on CD, vision aides, specialized equipment for the blind) that the library has available for use. The library can also create special institution library cards to enable the activity directors of the local assisted living centers or nursing homes to check out materials for residents to use.

OUT of the Library:

1. **Promote Awareness of Resources**: Library staff or members of the library's board can volunteer to speak about the Talking Books and Reading by Listening programs at school organizations, churches, and civic organizations to bring awareness to the resources. The librarian can also write a press release to make residents aware of these programs.
2. **Facilitate Access**: Library staff or representatives can take promotional brochures with information about the resources available at the library and through organizations such as Books Aloud, Inc., and the NLS to appropriate agencies, centers, and organizations in the community. They can include copies of the eligibility guidelines and application forms for the Talking Books and Reading by Listening programs along with informational handouts.
3. **Provide Materials to the Homebound**: The following is a simple outreach program a library can do to provide materials to those in assisted living centers, nursing homes, or long-term care facilities. The library contacts each potential partner facility to ask if it would like the library to deliver a small collection of books to residents on a monthly basis. For the facilities that want to partner with the library, each month a selection of large-print books, books on tape or CD, and players (cassette or CD depending on the situation) are delivered to them. Along with the collection is a sheet with the titles listed and a space next to each title for hash marks. The staff at the facility is responsible for handing the materials out to residents and recording a hash mark for each item used. Each month a new selection of materials is delivered, and the ones from the previous month are picked up. If more than one facility is participating, the packet of materials is taken to the next facility on the list.

When you give out the Library Roles Worksheet (2.8), include a brief cover letter describing why you are requesting the input, how you will use it, and the date by which you need the completed form. If it will help you in planning, include two or three survey questions, such as these:

- "Are you familiar with the library and services it offers?"
- "Have you used the library in the past year?"

- "Would you use the following service/resources if the library made them available?" (List the service or include a brief two- to three-sentence description of the project, program, resource, or service.)

Provide an easy way for the form to be returned, either by including a self-addressed, stamped envelope or by arranging to pick up the completed form by a specified date.

Compare the results of the forms you receive with the one you filled out (be sure to fill out your form before reading the ones you receive from other people). This will help you determine if there is a discrepancy between your perception of the library and that of the people in the community you serve.

Learning how members of the community view the library can be exhilarating, depressing, and enlightening all at the same time. Be prepared to be surprised.

Keep in mind that you do not have to do a formal survey of all the community. The purpose of the exercise is to serve as a check for you, a way to ensure you are not viewing the library through either rose-colored glasses or conversely through dark shades. Use Worksheet 2.8 to help you review your library's historical and current roles in the community along with working on what future role you would like the library to play.

WORKSHEET 2.8. LIBRARY ROLES: PAST, PRESENT, AND FUTURE

Below is a list of common roles of public libraries. Put an "H" by the ones your library has historically played in the community. Put a "C" by the ones the library currently fulfills. Put an "F" by ones you want it to play in the future.

Lifelong Learning	Adult Learning
Basic Literacy	Cultural Awareness
Free and Equal Access to Information	Current Topics and Titles
Community Meeting Place	Gateway to Information
Educational and Recreational Materials	Business Support
Technology Center	Public Computer Access
Information Assistance	Career and Workforce Development
English as a Second Language	Early Childhood Literacy
Local History and Genealogy	Community Commons
Formal Education Support	Heritage Center
Information Literacy	Preschool Door to Learning

List the roles here that you marked in the table.

Historical:

Current:

Future:

Outreach Needs and Assets Assessment

IN THIS CHAPTER:

Introduction

Traditionally public libraries have been perceived as a necessary element of a vital and vibrant community. Public libraries are viewed as an indicator of what makes a particular community attractive to existing and potential residents. This has not really changed. What has changed is how libraries need to do business to maintain that place in public perception, to attract additional financial support, and to weld more political clout in their local community. The library needs to be seen as a necessity rather than a nicety.

One change libraries need to make is to find out what their constituents want rather than deciding unilaterally what programs or services they want to offer to potential library users. Surveys and assessments can help you identify needs. They can also help verify what you believe is needed by a particular segment of your community's population. They provide a way to confirm your perceptions.

This is essentially a marketing approach. But we need to be clear about what we mean when we say "marketing." In the library world, "marketing" is often used as a synonym for "advertising" or "selling." Librarians use the term to describe efforts to create awareness about services they provide and to promote appreciation for the work they do. In the business world, trying to convince an individual or group to purchase the product or service that you make or provide is called "selling." Marketing, in contrast, is asking a group or individual what product or service that they want to buy and then developing a product or service that meets that identified demand.

Libraries would be well advised, therefore, to use marketing tools like focus groups and surveys to provide structured ways to listen to the communities they seek to serve. And while asking them what they like and do not like about the resources and service the library provides may prove useful, libraries also need to pursue truly deep inquiries into what the community needs and wants to improve their lives and then fashion programs and services that meet those needs and desires. For example, it is far less important to ask library users what hours they want the library to be open than it is to investigate what their goals and needs are and then think creatively about what we can do to help them achieve their goals or fulfill their needs. And we need to listen carefully for trends that affect our perceived value in the community and to take early steps to address shifts in those perceptions.

Needs Assessment

Definition: A needs assessment is a systematic process for collecting and analyzing information using one or more techniques.

Needs assessments are used to identify priorities, define results to be accomplished, guide decisions on appropriate actions to take, establish ways to evaluate actions taken to determine success, and help improve services and programs. Service and programming planning basically consists of answering four questions:

1. What do we offer now?
2. What do we want to offer?
3. How do we do that?
4. How do we measure our success?

A needs assessment helps you answer these questions.

Assets Assessment

Definition: An assets assessment provides a systematic way to inventory positive aspects of the community and library. The assets identified can be used to help you make positive decisions on how the library can better serve the community.

The asset assessment should be considered independent of but relevant to the needs assessment. When you are thinking about assets include attitudes of the staff, such as being friendly, helpful, or courteous. Consider talents, skills, interests, or associations that each member of the staff, volunteers, library board members, or members of the Friends of the Library may have, such as artistic ability; woodworking skills; kite builder; model train enthusiast; teaches etiquette; a wiz with social networking technologies; teaches computer skills classes; great at doing preschool storytime; has a parent in the local nursing home; is president of the local DAR, and so on. Include geographic and physical features that reflect positively on the community, such as seaside resort or mountain retreat. Local civic, social, service-oriented, and recreational organizations in addition to schools, hospitals, colleges, and vocational technical schools should all be included in your inventory. You might have groups such as a Red Hat Club, gardening club, a sorority, or honor society in town along with a Rotary, Optimist, or Lions Club. Be sure to include these in your assessment.

Needs and Assets Assessment

Many libraries conduct a needs and assets assessment in anticipation of a building project or as part of the process of putting together a technology plan. It is recognized that such an assessment is critical when planning for a new building or creating a technology plan. In a building assessment the focus is more on how much space is needed, use of the space, location of the building, potential staffing and collection levels, and other facility-related issues. A technology plan assessment might cover the type of existing wiring, Internet connections, computer workstations, broadband width, connection speed, computer usage, and Wi-Fi capabilities.

Similarly, conducting a needs and assets assessment for outreach in your community is a necessary step in developing an effective community outreach plan. When conducting a community outreach needs assessment the focus is on identifying unmet service needs and ways to fill those needs.

The resulting assessment will help you match the outreach needs identified with library and community assets that can meet those needs. A well-written outreach plan helps ensure programs and services meet the current and future needs of the community. For our purposes, we will use the following definition of outreach.

Outreach

Definition: Outreach programs or services are designed to connect, educate, and serve nontraditional or underserved communities and populations.

Bear in mind that community outreach can be focused on bringing new users into the library to provide services and resources that they need. But it can also be designed to take the library out into the community, working with other community organizations, to create and demonstrate value to the community. Underserved and unserved segments of the community can benefit from both types of outreach. Going out into the community can sometimes be a more effective way to raise awareness of the library, generate new users, and demonstrate public value.

If you are considering adding a new service or program, then you need to assess if there is a need for it and, if so, the level of that need. If you are reviewing an established service or program, then you need to evaluate what users think of that service or program and how it is being provided or delivered.

Together the needs and assets assessment will help you find answers to questions such as:

1. Are there groups in the community we are not reaching? If so, what groups?
2. Is the library the right organization to address the needs of this group? If so, does the library currently offer programs that could benefit this target group? If so, what are they?
3. To what extent are these programs or services successful with the target group? If these programs and services are not being used by the target group, why?
4. Are there new services or programs that might better meet the needs of the target group? If so, what are they?
5. Is there a way to make the library and its services more useful to the target group through community partnerships? If so, what

organizations and programs in the community might the library consider as partners?

6. What expectations does the target group have of the library? How can the library meet those expectations?
7. Are there additional materials or information the library and/or its partners could provide to better fill the need of the target group?
8. Do staffing patterns or library hours need to be adjusted to meet the needs of the target group?

You can use a number of methods to do a needs and assets assessment, and there are different components you can choose to include. For our assessment, we will include the following.

1. Geographical Information

For example, a ski or beach resort with a seasonal influx of tourists has different service needs than a community with a large population of migrant workers, even though each has a flux in population based on season. The geographical location within the community impacts library use, services provided, and programs offered. If the library is next door to a middle school, the number of children using the library after school will tend to be higher than if the middle school is five miles away. You identified a number of these factors in Worksheet 2.5 (pp. 18–20).

2. Demographic Data

This includes historical and current demographic data, such as population broken down by age, ethnic groups, education, languages spoken, and income. You identified some of these in Worksheet 2.7 (p. 28).

3. Statistical Data

Program attendance, interlibrary loan use, computer workstation use, and circulation statistics are helpful in ascertaining patterns of use. You identified some of these in Worksheet 2.7 (p. 28).

4. Economic Data

The community's primary economic base, major employers, unemployment figures, and poverty levels should be considered. For example, if the community's economy is primarily agricultural, with the main crops being cotton, corn, soybeans, and rice, then agriculture is the economic base and the major employers might be the local gin, mill, and megafarm. Worksheets 2.5 (pp. 18–20) and 2.7 (p. 28) included some of this information.

5. Social, Cultural, Educational, and Recreational Organizations

The assessment should include current information on religious and civic organizations, cultural organizations, recreational facilities, and communitywide special events. Information on special interest groups such as artists, genealogists, athletic organizations, veterans, hunters, gaming, sportsmen, boaters, gardeners, or quilters should be gathered. Worksheet 3.1 (p. 38) will help you do this.

IN & OUT: Program Ideas

Target Group: Homeschool Families

Program Types:

1. Host Homeschool Meetings
2. Develop Homeschool Resource Collection
3. Create Homeschool Resource Links for Website
4. Host a Homeschool Fair
5. Attend Homeschool Association Meeting
6. Literacy Kits for Long-Term Checkout

Potential Partners:

Bookstores, churches, community radio, television, and newspapers are potential partners for promoting materials, programs, and services the library has for families homeschooling their children. Placing brochures about homeschool resources in doctors' offices is another way to get the word out. Speaking at homeschool associations and homeschool support groups is a way to connect with this target group. Putting information about library resources in their newsletters and on their websites and sending information to local homeowners' associations and neighborhood associations for inclusion in their newsletters are all viable promotion techniques.

Resources:

1. The Bookwink website has video book talks on a variety of themes for children in third through eighth grades: http://www.bookwink.com.
2. *A Teacher's Guide to Folklife Resources for K–12 Classrooms* from the Library of Congress provides an extensive list of resources to help bring folklife into the classroom: http://www.loc.gov/folklife/teachers/index.html.
3. National Geographic's website for young readers is one of the best resources for information on the Internet about the world, its people, and its wildlife: http://www.nationalgeographic.com/kids/.
4. The Smithsonian Center for Folklife and Cultural Heritage has excellent cultural education programs and materials for K–12 teachers: http://www.folklife.si.edu/index.html.
5. United Nations Cyberschoolbus provides information about member nations. It is interactive and well designed for school-age children: http://www.un.org/pubs/cyberschoolbus/.

IN the Library:

1. **Host Homeschool Meetings**: Provide a place to meet at the library for local homeschool groups.
2. **Develop Homeschool Resource Collection**: Create an advisory committee composed of library staff and members of local homeschool groups in your community. Use their input along with online websites and recommended lists to develop a collection of how-to-homeschool materials. Create a brochure to publicize the materials. In addition to having the brochures available at the library, provide copies to local homeschool groups and submit it to be included in their newsletters.
3. **Create Homeschool Resource Links for Website**: Create a brochure listing resources available at the library for those who homeschool. Create a section on your library website with links to online resources such as the ones described earlier.
4. **Host a Homeschool Fair**: Sponsor a homeschool fair. Partner with the local bookstore, churches, and family agencies to provide information on resources available from each that can support the efforts of families who homeschool their children. Have the fair in the library meeting room and provide refreshments, tour of the library, demonstrate databases and available technology, and display materials the library has, such as literacy backpacks and tutorials on how to homeschool.

OUT of the Library:

1. **Attend Homeschool Association Meetings**: Go to the local homeschool association or support group meeting. Provide brochures of materials, including databases the library has available. If the library has literacy backpacks, take a couple with you to display. Take a laptop to do database demonstrations if wireless service is available at the meeting location.
2. **Literacy Kits for Long-Term Checkout**: Purchase a collection of pre-packaged literacy kits or make your own. If you make your own, you can package them in bags, backpacks, or other containers. You can find resources by searching the Internet. Search terms include literacy kits, story sacks, story bags, literacy bags, literacy backpacks, and discovery packs.

WORKSHEET 3.1. EXISTING AND POTENTIAL PARTNERS FOR COLLABORATION

EXISTING PARTNERS

In the table, list organizations, agencies, and individuals the library already partners with to provide services or programs.

Agencies/Organizations	Individuals with Specialized Skills

POTENTIAL PARTNERS

List the organizations, agencies, and individuals the library has not partnered with previously.

Agencies/Organizations	Individuals with Specialized Skills

IN & OUT: Program Ideas

Target Group: Intergenerational

Program Types:

1. Family and Community History
2. Genealogy
3. Gardening

Potential Partners:

Churches; senior citizens centers; genealogy societies; schools; master gardeners; county extension agents; gardening clubs; teen associations; Boy Scouts of America; Girl Scouts of the USA; Family, Career, and Community Leaders of America, Inc. (FCCLA); National FFA Organization; students in the National Honor Society; and other community service–oriented organizations and clubs are potential partners.

Resources:

1. The Smithsonian Center for Folklife and Cultural Heritage has downloadable lesson plans and learning guides. The Cultural Education webpages include videos, online exhibitions, and links to cultural heritage educational materials. One resource is the *Smithsonian Folklife and Oral History Interviewing Guide*: http://www.folklife.si.edu/education_exhibits/resources/guide/introduction.aspx.
2. Genwriters was created as a forum to bring together web-based and print resources to assist genealogists in writing their family histories. The website includes suggestions on how to get children involved in family history projects: http://www.genwriters.com/children.html.
3. The Boy Scouts of America have a merit badge in genealogy. The requirements can be found on the website: http://usscouts.org/mb/mb056.asp.
4. The USGenWeb website states: "The USGenWeb Project consists of a group of volunteers working together to provide Internet websites for genealogical research in every county and every state of the United States. The Project is non-commercial and fully committed to free access for everyone." It has a section for children called "USGenWebKidz." Genealogy forms, how-to information, and other resources are geared toward teens and younger children. It includes links to other useful sites: http://www.rootsweb.ancestry.com/~usgwkidz/link/howto.html.
5. The National Gardening Association website states: "For more than 35 years, the National Gardening Association (NGA) has been working to renew and sustain the essential connection between people, plants, and the environment. As a nonprofit leader in plant-based education, our vision is to make available free educational plant-based materials, grants, and resources that speak to young minds, educators, youth and community organizations, and the general gardening public in five core areas; education, health and wellness, environmental stewardship, community development, and home gardening. It includes a section for kids: http://www.kidsgardening.org/.
6. Kiddie Gardens: Gardens for Children & Gardening with Kids is a U.K.-based website. It has sections on gardening with kids; growing vegetables with kids; garden crafts for kids; projects you can do with a child to create a wildlife garden; learning activities; garden safety, and links to other resources: http://www.kiddiegardens.com.

IN the Library:

1. **Family History**: Host a program for families to celebrate Grandparents Day. Activities can include creating family folklore scrapbooks; compiling a book of family stories; and creating shadowboxes of memorabilia using photographs, copies of family documents, and other keepsakes.
2. **Genealogy**: Have a program on genealogy for children and their parents. The library can partner with the local genealogy society to provide demonstrations of free website resources, such as http://www.familysearch.org and http://www.cyndislist.com/. Provide copies of family forms for participants to use to begin recording their genealogy. Hold a follow-up program for families to make an illustrated family tree annotated with stories and reminiscences about different family members.

(Continued)

IN & OUT: Program Ideas ***(Continued)***

IN the Library ***(Continued)*****:**

3. **Gardening:** Ask a representative of a local gardening club, county extension agency, or master gardener to present a program for parents and children on gardening geared toward children.

OUT of the Library:

1. **Community History:** Facilitate an oral history project using teens to interview long-term residents of the community. Organizational and training meetings can be held at the library, with interviews taking place at the senior citizens centers, civic organizations like the Rotary, local historical commissions, a heritage society, or a museum. The teen participants could be from the Boy Scouts, Girl Scouts, FCCLA, National FFA Organization, and National Honor Society. The Smithsonian Center for Folklife and Cultural Heritage has a downloadable *Oral History Interviewing Guide* (http://www.folklife.si.edu/education_exhibits/resources/guide/introduction.aspx) that could be used for this program.
2. **Gardening:** As part of the Summer Reading Program have teens help young children to plant flowers in pots. Arrange for the teens and children to take the potted flowers to residents of the local nursing home or assisted living center.

6. Strengths and Weaknesses

As part of the needs and assets assessment, it is helpful to review the current strengths and weaknesses of the library and community. You may have conducted a full-blown SWOT (strengths, weaknesses, opportunities, and threats) assessment in the past. If so, now would be a good time to review it.

For the purpose of planning for outreach, however, we will not do a formal SWOT. Instead, we will use the assets (strengths) and weaknesses (challenges) information you identified when you completed Worksheets 2.5 (pp. 18–20) and 2.7 (p. 28).

Conducting a community needs analysis includes asking citizens specifically what their information needs and interests are and enables the library to design and provide more useful services. An analysis of the responses enables the library to identify current and future needs of the identified service population, rank the needs in order of importance, set goals and objectives to meet the needs, select and acquire appropriate material, design library services to address the identified needs, and help establish a case for financial support.

Research and feedback from customers can assist you in assessing and evaluating new or existing programs or services. Feedback can be elicited from those who govern, promote, use, or do not use the library. You can get feedback by distributing surveys through an ad in the local newspaper; newsletters; e-mail; websites (library, city, county, civic, and service organizations; chambers of commerce; etc.); presentations at local government, association, and organization meetings; or leaving a stack at the local post office, coffee shop, bakery, restaurants, and other popular spots around town. You can also interview community leaders, citizens, library users, and those who do not use the library.

The following worksheets can be used as is or modified as needed to help you perform your needs assessment:

- Worksheet 3.2 is a general needs survey dealing with hours of operation, types of programs offered, and types of programs desired.

WORKSHEET 3.2. GENERAL LIBRARY NEEDS SURVEY	
You can use this general survey for your needs assessment or modify it to more closely fit your specific situation.	
Do you know the location of the public library? ❑ Yes ❑ No	**What age group best describes you?** ❑ Over 50 ❑ 18–30 ❑ 31–50 ❑ 12–18
How often do you visit the library? ❑ Daily ❑ Twice a year ❑ Weekly ❑ Once a year ❑ Monthly ❑ Never	**Which best describes your marital status?** ❑ Single ❑ Widowed ❑ Married ❑ Divorced
Do you find the current hours to be convenient? ❑ Yes ❑ No	**If you have children, what are their ages?** ***(Check all that apply.)*** ❑ 0–2 years ❑ 6–12 years ❑ 3–5 years ❑ 13–17 years
If not, what hours would you like the library to be open?	**In what town or community do you live?**
What programs would you like the library to add or expand?	**For what age group would you like to see more programs?**
When are you most likely to use the library? ❑ Morning (8:00–noon) ❑ Afternoon (noon–5:00 p.m.) ❑ Evening (after 5:00 p.m.)	**Which days of the week would you be most likely to use the library?** ***(Check all that apply.)*** ❑ Monday ❑ Thursday ❑ Tuesday ❑ Friday ❑ Wednesday ❑ Saturday

- Worksheet 3.3 (p. 42) is a sample survey to use with your city or county management, library advisory or governing board, library friends group, and other community leaders.
- Worksheet 3.4 (p. 43) is a sample survey for a group you have identified as unserved or underserved.
- Worksheet 3.5 (p. 44) is a sample survey for you, your staff, and any library volunteers to complete.
- Worksheet 3.6 (p. 45) can be used to compile the results.

The assets assessment should center on the assets of your library and of the community relevant to meeting the service needs you identify. The assessment can help you determine how best to use the existing

(Continued p. 46)

WORKSHEET 3.3. NEEDS SURVEY FOR OFFICIALS AND LEADERS
You can use this survey as is or customize it for your library needs assessment.
What do you see as the major strengths of the library?
What do you see as the major weaknesses of the library?
List any groups of people who do not currently use the library that you want to attract.
What do you think the perception of the library is in the community?
What do you see as potential new partnerships for the library?
What community groups/organizations are potential partners for the library?
How would you rate the knowledge and customer service of the staff on a scale of 1–10 with 10 being the highest?
What types of programs are the most important to you?
What improvements would you like to see in the library collections?
Do you think the average resident is aware of the wide range of programs and services the library has to offer?
Do you have any suggestions for better marketing of the library?
Describe the perfect library for this community. What features would it have?

WORKSHEET 3.4. NEEDS SURVEY TARGET GROUPS
Modify this sample survey to customize it for your library needs assessment. You can use one for each group you are targeting or create custom ones for each group depending on the information you want to gather.
Do you know where the public library is located?
Have you or members of your family been to the library in the past six months?
If so, what was the reason for your visit?
Did you find what you were looking for?
What do you like about the library?
What do you not like about the library?
How would you rate the knowledge and customer service of the staff on a scale of 1–10 with 10 being the highest?
What types of programs are the most important to you?
What improvements would you like to see in the library collections?
Are there programs or services you would like the library to offer? If so, please list them.
If the library offered ____________________ *(fill in the blank)* service would you or other members of your family use it?
If the library offered ____________________ *(fill in the blank)* program would you or other members of your family attend it?

WORKSHEET 3.5. NEEDS SURVEY STAFF AND VOLUNTEERS
Modify this sample survey to customize it for your library needs assessment.
What do you see as the major strengths of the library?
What do you see as the major weaknesses of the library?
List the groups of people that currently use the library.
List any groups of people who do not currently use the library that you want to attract.
What do you think the perception of the library is in the community?
What community groups/organizations are potential partners for the library?
How would you rate the knowledge and customer service of the staff on a scale of 1–10, with 10 being the highest?
What types of programs are the most important to you?
What improvements would you like to see in the library collections?
Do you think the average resident is aware of the wide range of programs and services the library has to offer?
Do you have any suggestions for better marketing of the library?
Describe the perfect library for this community. What features would it have?
What changes have you noticed in the community in the past year? (Fewer or more of a particular category of user? More questions of a particular type?)

WORKSHEET 3.6. NEEDS COMPILATION	
Look at your completed Worksheets 2.5 and 2.7 and list the items you marked that you considered to be a challenge or need. Include the results of the needs surveys you distributed to the general public, officials, community leaders, and library staff and volunteers.	

assets of the library and community. This promotes the development of a meaningful, targeted outreach plan. Worksheet 3.7 can be used to help you ascertain library staff or volunteer assets. Worksheet 3.8 (p. 48) can be used to compile assets you have identified.

The desired outcomes for the assessment are the following:

- To help the library make informed decisions regarding what needs are not being met by the library and ways to meet them
- To help the library improve the quality of life in the community in clearly defined ways
- To make it possible for the library to serve a larger segment of the population
- To help the library to take a leadership role in meeting the needs of the citizens it serves
- To gain acknowledgment of the library as an important and relevant cornerstone of the community

In Chapter 2, you either wrote or reviewed your library's overall vision and mission statements, goals and objectives, and activities and action plans. You filled out worksheets to help you get a feel for the impact geographic, demographic, and statistical factors can have on your community and library services. You will use each of these components as you move forward with conducting a needs and assets assessment.

Potential Programs

Once you have written or reviewed the library's vision and mission statements and goals and objectives and completed your needs and assets assessment, it is time to look at potential programs. You want to consider what you learned through the assessment in light of the stated direction of the library. If you have an existing program or service that can be adapted to fill a need identified related to your unserved or underserved population, then concentrate on it. If you do not have a program or service in place that can be adapted, then consider what type of new program would fill the need. Worksheet 3.9 (p. 49) will help you with this.

Consider also whether or not the program or project is one that lends itself to partnership opportunities. Here are some questions to ask yourself to help you select an appropriate project and partners:

1. Does the proposed project meet an identified need in the community?
2. Does the proposed project fit in with the library's vision, mission, goals, and objectives?
3. Is there something about the project that would benefit from having a partner?
4. What kind of partner is needed (government, organization, institution, individual, or business)?

(Continued p. 50)

WORKSHEET 3.7. LIBRARY ASSETS OF STAFF

Below is a list of possible assets. Put an "A" by the ones you believe one or more of your library staff and/or volunteers possess.

Involved in community groups and organizations	Appreciate diversity
Good management skills	Good budgeting skills
Grant-writing experience	Fundraising skills
Good people skills	Ability to manage detailed projects
Staff works well together	Diverse staff
Staff have good computer skills	Staff are technology savvy
Form partnerships with other departments	Committed to encouraging early literacy
Advocate free and equal access to information	Collaborate with community partners to encourage early literacy
Reach out to provide services to those unable to visit the library	Collaborate with community partners to encourage adult literacy
Share knowledge and resources	Collaborate with community partners to offer ESL classes
Encourage feedback	Promote love of reading for all life stages/ages
Provide responsive service by listening to library users	Provide career and workforce development assistance
Identify trends	Maintain confidentiality of library user records
Professional staff	Communicate openly with each other and library users
Well-trained staff	Have citizenship classes
Have knowledgeable staff	Have a computer lab
Have friendly and helpful staff	Offer basic computer skills classes
Have bilingual staff	Skilled storyteller
Have experienced staff	Genealogist
Have enthusiastic staff	Staff has gaming experience

List the main assets that you marked in the table.

Assets:

WORKSHEET 3.8. ASSETS COMPILATION

Look at your completed Worksheets 2.5, 2.7, and 3.7. Enter below the ones you marked on those worksheets as a community or library asset.

Community	Library

WORKSHEET 3.9. POTENTIAL PROGRAMS

Common library programs are listed. Put a "P" (for potential) next to ones your library does not currently offer but could meet an unfilled need in your community. Use the blank spaces provided to list other programs that your library would like to offer to unserved or underserved segments of your population.

Regular Lap Sit Program	Regular Toddler Storytime
Regular Storytime for Preschool	Regular Storytime for Day Care Centers
Summer Reading Program for Children	Summer Reading Program for Teens
Winter Reading Program for Children	Canned Food Drive
Adult Book Club	Adult Reading Program
Family Literacy Program	Teen Book Club
Work Skills Assistance (classes/program)	Regular Family Film/Fun Night
Spanish Language Classes	Homeschool Programs
Regular Computer Gaming Programs	English Language Classes
Basic Computer Literacy Classes	Regular Gaming Programs
Nursing Home Outreach	Assisted Living Center Outreach
Homebound Outreach	Migrant Outreach
Outreach to Homeless	Regular Author Visits
Regular Lecture Series	English as a Second Language
GED Preparation Tutoring	Exam Proctoring
Literacy Program with Tutors and Students	Interlibrary Loan
Preparation for Citizenship Classes	Storytime Programs in Spanish
Teen Blog (maintained by library staff)	Scrapbooking with Library Dies
Library Wiki (maintained by library staff)	Memory Books for Teens
Regular Art Displays	Regular Genealogy Programs
Project to Create Photo Archive of Local Importance	Digitalizing Local History
Digitalizing Local History Photo Archive	Digitalizing Local Newspaper
Digitalizing Local Government	Digitalizing Local Cemetery Gravestones
Digitalizing Local Church Historical Records	Digitalizing Local Funeral Home Records
Digitalizing Local Cemetery Records	Digitalizing Local Obituaries

Programs to consider to meet (insert identified need):

Programs to consider to meet (insert identified need):

Programs to consider to meet (insert identified need):

5. What does the library have to offer to the partnership?
6. What would a partner have to offer?
7. What kind of partnership would this be (money, sponsorship, volunteers, or in-kind donation)?
8. What would be the benefit to each party?
9. How much time and effort is required to bring interested people on board?
10. Is the project and partnership cost-effective?

Potential Partners

Another way libraries need to change how they do business is to embrace a changing paradigm of service. In the past the library approach was to primarily provide materials and resources within the walls of the library. This way of doing business depended on the librarian and/or library staff's knowledge of the collection and library services. It was insular and operated to a large degree independently of the community as a whole.

Libraries need to shift focus. Rather than expecting people to come to the library for resources, the library must reach out to the community to make resources available. The focus shifts to providing the resources and services that best meet the needs of their constituency regardless of where or how that service or resource is provided.

Many libraries have done this to a certain degree by utilizing technological tools such as websites, wikis, blogs, e-books, database resources, and e-mail reference. However, these are still, to a great extent, insular. It is the library website, wiki, or blog. And the library chooses the e-books and databases to make available.

Partnering with others in the community can provide you with additional resources and deepen community commitment to your library as it deepens the library's commitment to the community. It can create a higher profile for the library and increase positive feelings about the library's value to the community. It can help the library get the input it needs to be able to truly provide what is wanted in the community. It improves the library's position with influential community leaders and decision makers. This in turn can help secure support, funding, sponsorships, volunteers, and in-kind donations to implement new programs and services.

By partnering with other organizations or groups, the library can reach out to those who need the resources the library has to offer. Collaboration enables the library to provide services in the best method possible even if it means going outside the library walls. The focus shifts from the librarian's knowledge of the library collection and services to the librarian's knowledge of the community agencies and the resources available through them. It is a looking outward rather than looking inward mentality.

These are some benefits of partnering:

IN & OUT: Program Ideas

Target Group: Adults

Program Types:

1. Adult Summer Reading Program
2. Adult Book Club
3. Lunch Book Talk Series
4. Author Series
5. Lecture Series

Potential Partners:

Local businesses, bookstores, churches, senior citizens centers, chambers of commerce, civic organizations, neighborhood associations, homeowner associations, and literary organizations are all potential partners. Recruit participants, volunteers, and sponsors, and request donations to support your adult program from these potential partners. The community radio, television, and newspaper are good outlets to use to promote your program. Don't forget to post the information in the library and on the library website. You can include the information in the local parks and recreation guide and on the city and/or county websites. You may be able to include the information in the chamber of commerce's newsletter or website listing for events. Sending an e-mail notification and posting the information on the library's Facebook site or blog are other ways to publicize the program.

IN the Library:

In the library, hold any of the programs listed above under Program Types. Because these are fairly traditional adult programs offered by libraries, we will not go into further detail.

OUT of the Library:

1. **Adult Summer or Winter Reading Program:** Hold registration for an Adult Summer or Winter Reading Program at local churches, businesses, and meetings of civic or homeowner associations. Have registration at local celebrations prior to the starting date of the reading program.
2. **Adult Book Club**: Partner with a local new or used bookstore to have a joint Adult Book Club project. Hold one meeting at the library and the next at the bookstore. Negotiate discount rates for the library to purchase multiple copies of the book to be read or to provide a discounted rate to participants if they will be purchasing their own copy of the book.
3. **Lunch Book Talk Series**: Partner with local restaurants to have a Lunch Book Talk Series. Do a once a month book talk at local restaurants on a rotational basis. Negotiate a special lunch discount for participants.
4. **Author or Lecture Series**: Partner with a local bookstore, restaurant, museum, community center, chamber of commerce, church, or civic organization. Have the partner host the program; the library makes author arrangements. Expenses can be shared.

- Reducing duplication of effort
- Expanding the resources and services available to library users
- Utilizing existing professional skills and experience of others
- Making better use of limited funds, staff, and time
- Helping the library receive more money or in-kind donations
- Creating a higher profile of the library in the community
- Improving the library's stock with influential members of the community
- Projecting a more positive image to stakeholders

When considering a partnership with a particular organization or agency, ask yourself these basic questions:

1. What is the purpose of the proposed partnership?
2. Is the proposed partnership a good fit for both parties?
3. What type of partnership is being considered?
4. What will the library provide, and what will the partner provide; for example, money, sponsorship, expertise, in-kind donation, volunteers, or use of facility?
5. How much staff time will be required by both parties?
6. What is the cost/benefit to each party?
7. Should a problem arise between the two parties, how will it be handled?

By considering questions such as these ahead of time you will be in a better position to approach your potential partner to propose a collaboration. Do your research beforehand so that when you do try to recruit partners you will already know whether your proposed program or project is one they would be interested in funding, sponsoring, or assisting with in other ways.

Community-Centered Library

The goal is to become a community-centered library. Often the library proceeds from the point of view of the library and its needs, wants, and priorities. The community-centered library thinks about the community's needs, wants, and priorities.

Characteristics of a community-centered library include the following:

1. The library's priority is on providing services to the individuals, organizations, businesses, and institutions in the community.
2. The library recognizes it exists because of the community and for the community.
3. The library staff know people, not things, come first.
4. The library actively solicits input from various segments of the community.
5. The library facilitates partnerships between it and other agencies or between citizen groups and appropriate organizations.
6. Partnerships are beneficial to both the library and the partner.

Let's look at some examples of a mutually beneficial partnership.

Example 1: Supporting Bilingual Literacy in Schools

The local elementary school has a high number of Hispanic children. The public library provides a selection of age-appropriate bilingual children's books to the school librarian each week. The school librarian uses the books to offer a regular bilingual storytime. In return, she agrees to send Spanish/English promotional pieces about the public library home with each child whenever the library requests her to do so. The public

IN & OUT: Program Ideas

Target Group: Spanish-Speaking Adults and Children

Program Types:

1. Bilingual Signage
2. Bilingual Collection
3. Bilingual Storytime
4. Early Childhood Literacy

Potential Partners:

The library could partner with the local Spanish-language radio, television, and newspaper outlets to promote library services and programs. Family service agencies that work with Spanish-speaking clients, churches serving Hispanic populations, and local schools are potential partners.

Resources:

1. America Reads Spanish is a website resource for materials in Spanish. According to the website: "The Spanish Institute for Foreign Trade (ICEX) and the Spanish Association of Publishers Guilds (FGEE) have developed the campaign America Reads Spanish, aimed to increase the use and reading of our language through the thousands of libraries, schools and book stores of the US." It has two handy free downloadable publications titled *Librarian's 500 Top Picks: The Core Spanish Collection* and *The Core Spanish Collection for Children and Young Adults*. There are also new releases, bestsellers, and book reviews: http://www.americareadsspanish.org/.
2. REFORMA: The National Association to Promote Library and Information Services to Latinos and the Spanish-Speaking website has resources for libraries to use with Spanish-speaking patrons. The following information is from the website: "Established in 1971 as an affiliate of the American Library Association (ALA), REFORMA has actively sought to promote the development of library collections to include Spanish-language and Latino oriented materials; the recruitment of more bilingual and bicultural library professionals and support staff; the development of library services and programs that meet the needs of the Latino community; the establishment of a national information and support network among individuals who share our goals; the education of the U.S. Latino population in regards to the availability and types of library services; and lobbying efforts to preserve existing library resource centers serving the interests of Latinos." Resources for children and young adult services include websites in Spanish for children; bilingual storytime; online resources for librarians working with Latino children, and a Latino Young Adult bibliography: http://www.reforma.org/.
3. Colorín Colorado is a bilingual website for parents and educators who wish to help children become successful lifelong readers: http://www.colorincolorado.org.
4. International Digital Children's Library has books to read from around the world. According to the website: "The International Children's Digital Library (ICDL) is a research project funded primarily by the National Science Foundation (NSF), the Institute for Museum and Library Services (IMLS), and Microsoft Research to create a digital library of outstanding children's books from all over the world . . . all presented in the original languages in which they were published. . . . " There are hundreds of books in 29 different languages: http://www.childrenslibrary.org/.
5. Leading to Reading is an early literacy website available in English and Spanish. Young children can read, sing, play, and explore a variety of subjects and books: http://www.rif.org/leadingtoreading/en/.
6. Storyplace en Español is a Spanish-language website produced by the Charlotte Mecklenburg Library in North Carolina that offers online stories, booklists, and activities to do at home or on the Internet: http://www.storyplace.org/sp/storyplace.asp.

IN the Library:

1. **Bilingual Signage**: Partner with local leaders in the Hispanic community to develop bilingual signage for use in the library.
2. **Bilingual Collection**: Use online resources such as America Reads Spanish and REFORMA along with input from Spanish-speaking members of the community to develop or expand the library's collection of Spanish/English bilingual materials.
3. **Bilingual Links:** Add links to online resources such as the International Digital Children's Library to expand the children's materials you offer in Spanish. Have programs at the library to demonstrate how to use these websites.

(Continued)

IN & OUT: Program Ideas *(Continued)*

IN the Library *(Continued)*:

4. **Bilingual Collection**: Have displays of bilingual books along with bilingual brochures to promote the library's collection. Ask a local bilingual-speaking resident to translate into Spanish the promotional flyer, poster, brochures, or signs you create about the display.
5. **Bilingual Storytime**: Have monthly or weekly bilingual storytimes for families. Use online resources such as Storyplace en Español to have a simple storytime. Partner with a local bilingual-speaking resident to select and present a storytime centered around listening to one of the stories on Storyplace en Español. Basically you would select the story, set the time for the program, and publicize it. On the day of the program, you would have a large-screen monitor set up, comfortable seating for adults and children, and refreshments. The bilingual volunteer (or staff member if you have one) would welcome the participants, introduce the story, and start it. Afterward you could have a simple craft that parents could help their children do.

OUT of the Library:

1. **Bilingual Storytime**: You can simply modify the bilingual storytime program designed for in the library to do at local churches or day care centers with a high number of Spanish-speaking children. To do the program remotely, take a laptop, projector, and screen to the church or facility. Use online resources such as Storyplace en Español for an audio story. Partner with a local bilingual-speaking resident to select and introduce the storytime. Have a simple craft after the story.
2. **Bilingual Storytime**: Take a laptop, projector, and screen to the church or facility to project a bilingual book on a website such as International Digital Children's Library. Have a Spanish-speaking staff member or volunteer read the book aloud while showing the electronic page on the screen. *Angels ride bikes and other fall poems = Los ángeles andan en bicicleta y otros poemas de otoño* by Francisco X. Alarcón (San Francisco: Children's Book Press) published in 1999 is an example of a bilingual book available to read online at the International Digital Children's Library website.
3. **Early Childhood Literacy**: Partner with local churches and/or agencies serving Hispanic families in your service area. Ask to do a presentation at the church or facility for families on the importance of reading to young children. Design the program to help Hispanic parents become aware of the many resources the library has to help them increase their children's reading skills.

   As part of the program, provide a brochure written in Spanish listing the services and programs available for them at the library. Provide a bibliography of bilingual books the library has available for different age groups. Serve refreshments and have a display of some of the bilingual books. During the program, read one or more bilingual children's books. Through the program, the parents will learn why it is important to read to their young children and will learn through role modeling of the presenter how much fun it can be to read to and with their child.

library helps support the literacy of bilingual children and reaches their parents and families with targeted promotions about its Spanish programs and materials.

Example 2: Providing Bilingual Computer Classes for Workers

The library contacts the local workforce commission to find out if basic computer skills classes in Spanish would benefit residents who are unemployed. The commission does not have data to answer the question but agrees to work with the library to gather the data. The library provides a simple survey; the commission hands it out and gathers completed forms. It is determined there is a need. The library develops a basic computer skills class in Spanish with a bilingual instructor. The library provides brochures, flyers, posters, and bookmarks in Spanish and English to promote the program. The workforce commission promotes the program to Spanish-speaking job hunters.

Example 3: Promoting the Library to At-Risk Youth

There is an at-risk youth class at the local middle school of predominantly Spanish-speaking students. The library contacts the school and offers to host a "get to know your library" lunch program to be held on a Saturday for the students and parents to help them learn about the resources available to them at the public library. The library gets a local bakery, grocery store, and restaurant to donate food for a lunch for participants. It gets the local Optimist Club to donate backpacks to be given to each participating student. It gets the Friends of the Library to purchase paperback copies of a popular teen book in Spanish as well as a number in English. The school provides the Spanish/English flyer advertising the free lunch, backpacks, and books, along with the registration form, to each at-risk student. It gathers the completed forms and gives them to the library. At the lunch, students receive a backpack with a book. The library surveys the parents and students after the program to find out if there are specific services or programs they want, such as ESL classes, structured after-school homework help, tutoring help, or set times to use the library computers for homework.

Making the Pitch

Once you have identified a potential partner, you need to make the pitch. This is where you get your counterpart at the other organization or business to buy into the project. You need to be ready to show why it would want to partner with you. To do so, be ready to make a presentation to the board, chairman, or members of the other organization. When you do make your presentation, if at all possible, take other committed stakeholders with you. This might be a member of the library board, library friends group, a spokesperson for the target group, or a member of another organization sponsoring or partnering with you on the project.

Prepare materials that show what group you are targeting, how the group was identified, why the program was selected, and how it will help the group. It is best to keep this short and to the point.

Prepare an easy to read and understand flyer, chart, or brochure to get the main points across. Be sure that when you ask for what you want (time, money, resources, manpower, etc.) you are specific. At the same time, leave an opening for a variety of responses. Ask in such a way that it leaves the other person options of how he or she can partner with you.

Tips for Making the Pitch

Before approaching a potential partner, get prepared:

- Know what you want, and why.
- Prepare your message carefully.
- Keep in mind your audience.
- Do your research; match desired outcome with your potential partner's interests or concerns.

- Be ready to show the other person why he or she would want to be a partner.
- Have documentation prepared showing what groups of people in the community would benefit from the program or project. Include statistics, survey results, and any other background materials.

Once you have made your preparations, call in advance to set up the meeting. Be sure to identify yourself and the library, be polite, and ask to meet when and where it is convenient for the other person.

At the meeting make sure you know your facts. Be specific and remember to ask for collaboration in a way that allows multiple possible positive responses. Keep the meeting short, to the point, positive, and interesting. One of the most important things you can do is to listen carefully. This will help you determine what the concerns are of the other person as well as identify any special areas of interest you may have missed when you were doing your research. As you are listening, try to anticipate objections and be prepared to counter them. Have positive expectations, and project this. Indicate it by using statements such as, "I am sure we can work together. I believe we can find a way to collaborate on this project that will benefit both the library and your organization." Be sure to establish when you can expect an answer. Once you have made your pitch and established when and how you will hear back from the person, do not linger. Follow up with a thank-you note to the person to express your appreciation for his or her time.

Outreach Plan

IN THIS CHAPTER:

- ✔ Introduction
- ✔ Community Profile Narrative
- ✔ Library Profile Narrative
- ✔ Vision, Mission, Goals, and Objectives
- ✔ Outreach Programs
- ✔ Detailed Action Plan
- ✔ Appendix (Optional)

Introduction

The outreach plan template is designed to provide structure while maintaining flexibility. Although public libraries are similar in certain respects, each is also unique based on factors such as community location and demographics, library focus, staff, and resources.

Writing an outreach plan is easy yet difficult. It is easy because of the planning you did in Chapters 2 and 3. It is difficult because you have to interpret the results and make decisions based on the library's focus and the data you have gathered. You have to turn what you learned into a meaningful, coherent plan.

The outreach plan includes: cover page; table of contents; introduction; community profile narrative; library profile narrative; vision, mission, goals, objectives; outreach program(s); and detailed action plan(s).

Cover Page

The cover page should include the name of the library, library's address, preparer's name, date the outreach plan was written, and other information you consider relevant such as website address, telephone number or fax telephone number. Worksheet 4.1 (p. 58) provides a template that you can modify for your own needs.

Table of Contents

The table of contents should include the major parts of your outreach plan. This makes it easier for others to know where to look for specific parts of the plan. Include the following: introduction; community profile narrative; library profile narrative; vision, mission, goals, objectives; outreach program(s), detailed action plan(s), and appendix items such as sample surveys, needs assessment, assets assessment, evaluation forms, or guidelines. Worksheet 4.2 (p. 58) provides a template that you can modify as needed.

WORKSHEET 4.1. COVER PAGE

COMMUNITY OUTREACH PLAN
FOR THE
______________ *(Insert Name)* LIBRARY

(You can insert a photo of your library here.)

Prepared by:

Date:

Library Street Address
City, State, Zip Code
Library Telephone Number
Library Website Address

WORKSHEET 4.2. TABLE OF CONTENTS

TABLE OF CONTENTS

(Remember to insert page numbers in place of the asterisks after you have completed writing your plan.)

Introduction

Write a brief paragraph or two that tells the reader where your community is located. Think in terms of someone trying to find your city and/or county on a map. Add some distinguishing features of your city or county, such as its population or perhaps how each was named. Include the following headings and information:

- Historical, Current, and Future Roles of the Library (from Worksheet 2.8, p. 31)
- Existing Programs (from Worksheet 2.6, p. 25)
- Identified Needs (from Worksheet 3.5, p. 44)
- Identified Assets (from Worksheet 3.7, p. 47)

You may want to include a thank-you after the introduction. Your governing entity (city, county, board of trustees), staff, volunteers, library advisory board, and library friends groups are people to consider thanking. If certain individuals or organizations make major contributions on a regular basis to your library, including a thank-you here would be appropriate.

Community Profile Narrative

This section is where you will introduce your community to the reader. The point of the community profile is to provide a picture of the social, economic, demographic, and geographic features of your community that can help you see patterns indicating challenges and opportunities.

Describe your community in a few paragraphs. Think of what you would tell someone planning a visit to your city or county, such as where museums, historical sites, or other buildings are located. Are there festivals or other special events held during the year? If so, tell a little something about these.

In addition, give the reader a flavor of what life is like in your community. Is it family oriented? Is it a bedroom community? If so, where do people go for work? Do people work primarily for one or two major employers in town? If so, name the employers (such as the local hospital or independent school district). Include the following headings:

- Main Geographic Features (from Worksheet 2.5, pp. 18–20)
- Community Demographics (from Worksheet 2.7, p. 28)

Example of a Community Profile Narrative

Residents of Our Town have historically been ranchers and the people who work for them. They depend on the land and livestock for their livelihood. Oil wells can also be found in the area. Our Town is the county seat of Our County and is located in a relatively isolated area. Our County consists of two towns, Our Town with a population of 2,121 and Other Town with a population of 4,698. Population density in the county is 1.9 persons per square mile. The nearest towns are located in counties other than our county. Neighboring Town is 28 miles away (population 6,000) and Other Neighboring Town is 22 miles away (population about 1,500). The nearest city with a population of 50,000 or more is approximately 170 miles.

Our County has a total population of 7,470, with 29.7 percent under 17 years and 16.4 percent over 65 years. The median age is 36.5. Approximately 21.3 percent of all ages live below the poverty line, with 31.9 percent of those under 18 years living in poverty. Approximately 44.7 percent of those aged 25+ years have a high school education, with 11.7 percent having a bachelor's degree or higher. The unemployment rate is 16.7 percent. The median value of homes in the county is $35,500, with the median household income being $27,490.

Nearly 97.8 percent of the population is White, with 83.3 percent of Hispanic or Latino origin; 1.2 percent of the population is African American, and 35.8 percent is foreign born. In 84.4 percent of the homes a language other than English is spoken.

The nearest commercial airport is 192 miles away. Our Town and Other Town each has a small municipal airport where private planes can land. Our Town also has a glider company based at the airport and is a destination for gliding enthusiasts because of the excellent thermals in the area. A number of ranches have private airstrips.

There are no hospitals in Our County. Our Town does have a community medical clinic. The closest hospital is located 28 miles

> away in Neighboring Town. There is no pharmacy, dentist, doctor, or drugstore in Our Town. There are no institutions of higher learning in Our Town; however, there is a state university in Neighboring Town.
>
> Our Town has an internationally known contemporary art museum; two foundations; a local history museum; a privately owned theater that occasionally presents plays, and a public radio station. There are a number of high-end art galleries and a Dollar General store.
>
> Various festivals are held throughout the year, including an art weekend, a film festival, a glider weekend, and a mystery lights festival held over Labor Day weekend. There are three hotels, two upscale and one more affordable, as well as a number of daily, weekly, and monthly short-term rental options. There are a number of eateries, including three fine dining, three cafés, two pizza places, two Mexican food places, and one Dairy Queen (fast food). In addition, two other establishments are occasionally open. There are two bars and one liquor store in town.

When you read a profile like this one, it should be obvious that some of the challenges of this particular community are isolation, low population density, unemployment, high number of people speaking a language other than English, low income, high poverty, low education, and few job opportunities. There are also indications of a dichotomy in economic status, with high-end art galleries, upscale hotels, and fine dining yet high poverty, high unemployment, and low education levels.

It would indicate the political and socioeconomic makeup of the community has changed from a primarily ranching community to a mixed one of ranching, art, and tourism. The possibility that there is an influx of newcomers to the area with higher incomes and educational levels is also indicated.

The library may need to develop two distinct sets of programs. One set for the majority of residents would focus on development of job skills, how to conduct a job search, how to improve one's education through distance learning, and English language skills. A second set of programs would be for the more educated, higher income residents on, for example, developing marketing plans, branding, and attracting niche shoppers.

The big picture is that the library can help the more affluent and educated segment of the population to attract more businesses to town, which creates a need for workers. At the same time, the library can help the local workforce develop the skills needed to qualify for the jobs created by the affluent segment of the population. The library can partner with other organizations in the region to provide these opportunities.

The results of the library's needs assessment would provide data on whether or not the analysis of potential programs is accurate or not based on what residents in the community actually indicate they want the library to provide.

IN & OUT: Program Ideas

Target Group: Job Seekers

Program Types:

1. Promote Awareness of Resources
2. Coffee and a Program Series
3. Workshops

Potential Partners:

Potential partners include the workforce commission, a community college, vocational-technical schools, churches, banks, local businesses and agencies, senior citizens centers, and ESL organizations.

IN the Library:

1. **Promote Awareness of Resources:** The library can promote resources available to help people looking for a job in a number of ways. These include book displays; bibliographies; website links on library computers; a website section devoted to job searching and developing skills; and handouts with tips for interviewing, writing a résumé, and conducting a job search.
2. **Coffee and a Program Series:** Have a weekly coffee and a program series featuring a mix of life skills–oriented presentations well as those directly related to finding a job. Possible topics include stress management; reducing credit card debt; telephone interview tips; ways to live on a restricted income; how to create and use a family spending budget; using Skype for video interviews; tips for saving on groceries, utilities, and medical expenses; job search skills; interview techniques; tips on résumé writing; and how to reduce car, life, and home insurance costs.
3. **Workshops:** Host a series of workshops on basic computer skills specifically geared for job seekers, including how to write or improve a résumé and how to handle a job interview. Partner with a local human resources professional (hospital, county offices, city department, or from a large employer) to hold an interview skills workshop. Recruit local senior citizens to serve as interviewers for participants to practice the skills they learn in the workshop.

OUT of the Library:

1. **Promote Awareness of Resources:** Have a table or booth at local job fairs offering handouts on the resources available at the library for job seekers. Give demonstrations of video conference–style interviews using Skype or on techniques to use when conducting a job search on the Internet.
2. **Facilitate Unemployment Services and Benefits Workshop:** Work with the local workforce commission and college to facilitate a workshop on the services and benefits available to unemployed workers. The workshop can be promoted at the library, on the library website, and to job seekers using the library at the agency and the college. The program itself could be held at the college with a representative from the agency and the college as the speakers. The library would provide handouts of resources available at the local public library. The agency can explain what is available through its office, and the college can talk about transferable skills.
3. **Facilitate Training Opportunities Workshop:** Partner with the local community college or vocational-technical school to facilitate a workshop about training opportunities. Hold the workshop on the college or school campus. The public library would promote the program and provide handouts on resources.
4. **Facilitate Job-Related ESL Programs:** Partner with ESL organizations to offer workshops for those learning English. Focus on words and terms specifically related to job search, application completion, and interview questions.

Library Profile Narrative

The library profile narrative should give the reader a sense of the library itself. It should include information such as a brief history of the library, sizes of the facility and collection, number of hours the library is open, staffing levels, and budget. You may write as much or little as you feel is necessary. Use information from Worksheets 2.5 (pp. 18–20) and 2.7 (p. 28) in your narrative.

Example of a Library Profile Narrative

> Our Town Public Library opened in 1973 and was remodeled in 2009. It is open 44 hours per week and has three full-time non-professional staff. The library has a collection of 20,035 items, with a circulation of 19,276 and 19,033 library visits annually. There are 2,709 cardholders. The library budget is $106,313, and the facility is 5,040 square feet with a small film auditorium sharing the library space. There is a six-person advisory board and a Friends of the Library group.

When you read a library profile like this one, it gives you an idea of the resources the library has available, such as budget, space, collection, and staffing. It also indicates potential supporters of and volunteers for the library (advisory board and friends group). In this case, it also tells you of a unique shared space in the library (the film auditorium).

Vision, Mission, Goals, and Objectives

In Chapter 2, you recorded your library's vision (Worksheet 2.1, p. 13), mission (Worksheet 2.2, p. 14), and goals and objectives (Worksheet 2.3, pp. 15–16). Transfer them to this part of your outreach plan.

Outreach Programs

In Chapter 3, you worked on a needs and assets assessment along with potential programs and partners. In this part you will consider the planning and findings from the assessment to formulate an appropriate library response. This is where you decide upon and design the program, project, or service you will implement to meet the needs you identified. You can use Worksheet 4.3 for this part of your plan.

It can be helpful to see how the process works. In the following example, a library with a middle school across the street is used.

Example of a Selected Program

> Many young teens visit the library after school but without any real focus or direction. The library is simply a place to hang out until it closes at 5:00 p.m. The library does have five computers for public use with a 30-minute time limit. There is usually a waiting list to use the computers. The library believes there is a need for teen programs to serve this group.
>
> A survey was designed to poll local teens to confirm the need and help the library determine how best to meet the need for teen programs. The library partnered with a local middle school to survey teens in the school. The survey consisted of questions such as:

WORKSHEET 4.3. MATCHING THE NEED, PROGRAM, AND POTENTIAL PARTNERS

List identified service or program needs in the first column. In the second column put existing or potential new library programs or services that could help fill the need. In the third column list any and all potential partners for the project.

Need	Program	Potential Partners

1. Where do you normally go after school?
2. What type of activities do you do after school?
3. Do you do your homework at home?
4. Do you have a computer at home?
5. Do you often go to the library after school?
6. Do you use the computers at the library?
7. Would you use the library if it was open later than 5:00 p.m.?
8. If the library provided computer time for homework would you use it?
9. If the library provided tutoring help would you use it?
10. If the library provided homework help would you use it?
11. What kind of programs would you like the library to offer for your age group?

IN & OUT: Program Ideas

Target Group: Schools

Program Types:

1. After-School Tutoring
2. After-School Homework Center
3. Accelerated Reader Support
4. GED Preparation
5. Summer Reading Program Outreach

Potential Partners:

Potential partners include local schools, media outlets, churches, a retired teachers' association, a community college, civic organizations, senior citizens centers, and businesses.

IN the Library:

1. **After-School Tutoring:** Work with the local schools to provide after-school tutoring at the library for students. The students can be self-selected or issued invitations to take part in the program. Tutors can be recruited from churches, a retired teachers' association, a community college, civic organizations, or senior citizens centers.
2. **After-School Homework Center:** Create an after-school homework center in the library. The center could consist of comfortable chairs, inexpensive snacks, and dedicated computer stations to be used only for homework research or word processing to type up papers and reports. Adult volunteers could monitor computer use and enforce time restrictions on use, check the computers in and out to students, and suggest resources.
3. **Accelerated Reader Support:** Work with the local schools to have a copy of the Accelerated Reading List available for students to use at the library.
4. **Summer Reading Program Outreach:** Contact the local schools to arrange for promotion of the Summer Reading Program. The library might provide flyers and bookmarks to be distributed to the students.

OUT of the Library:

1. **GED Preparation:** Partner with local schools, community colleges, or other organizations that provide GED classes. The public library could have copies of GED materials available in a special Learning Center at the library. The materials would be for use in the library and might include lessons on DVD as well as in book format. A dedicated computer with headphones could be a part of the Learning Center. Adult volunteers could be on hand during set hours to assist any GED students.
2. **Summer Reading Program Outreach:** Partner with the local school librarian to provide a Summer Reading Program for students in summer school. The public library could provide promotional posters, bookmarks, flyers, reading logs, and incentives to the school librarian. The school librarian could administer the program, and students could read books from the school library's collection. The public library could add the names of the students to any drawings held for prizes. In addition, the students could be invited to participate in an award ceremony held at the public library to receive their reading certificates, or a separate end of the Summer Reading Program event could be held at the school library.

Sixty surveys were handed out; 43 were returned. Ten indicated they had a computer at home and used it for homework. Thirty-three indicated they did not have a computer at home and would use the library computers for homework if there was a dedicated time to do so. Twenty indicated they would like tutoring help, and 19 would like homework help. Of the 43, 15 indicated they would like to have snacks at the library and would like to have games to play.

The library partnered with the local Rotary, Optimist, and Women's Clubs to recruit volunteers to provide homework help and tutoring twice a week at the library. The library requested and was approved to stay open until 7:00 p.m. twice a week to provide programs for homework help and tutoring. During those two hours, the library was not open to the general public, only to teens to use for homework, tutoring, and computer time. The teens were required to sign up for computer time, with a maximum of one hour each unless no one needed it. During the first 6 months, an average of 30 teens participated each night.

The library also instituted an after-school board game time from 3:00 to 5:00 p.m. with popcorn and lemonade one day a week. It was well attended, with an average of 13 teens a week.

As you do your analysis you may learn the need you thought existed did not. You may also identify a need you did not expect. Or you may realize there is no real interest in the program or service you were interested in offering. If that is the case, it is best to lay aside any plans you may have had for such a program. Otherwise, it will not be successful and will simply be a waste of time, money, and resources.

Interpreting the results can also lead to multiple program opportunities. Below is an example of how results can provide multiple program possibilities.

Examples of Multiple Program Opportunities

1. The Anytown Public Library's demographic data showed a high percentage of preschool-aged children. This indicated there might be a need for programs for this age group. After further research, the library staff learned there was a correspondingly high number of well-attended preschools and day cares in town. The staff recognized this necessitated a change in thinking and modified the library's response based on the actual needs. Instead of offering a weekly preschool storytime at the library as originally intended, the library provided support to the preschools and day cares. They developed a special collection of children's books that are delivered on a rotational basis to these agencies.

   An alternate response might be for the library to create a program to fill a niche market in the community. Knowing many preschool children are in day care or preschool facilities, the library might design and market a weekly preschool storyhour for the children of stay-at-home moms or dads, grandparents, or other caretakers. The program would require the adult to stay with the child during the program and would be promoted

IN & OUT: Program Ideas

Target Groups: Children in Day Care and Mother's Day Out Centers

Program Types:

1. Storytime
2. Summer Reading Program
3. Literacy Kits

Potential Partners:

Day care centers, Mother's Day Out centers, and local media outlets are potential partners.

Resources:

There are a number of websites and resource books one can use to enrich storytime or summer reading programs.

1. The Nellie Edge website states: "Nellie Edge is a kindergarten teacher, researcher, literacy coach, nationally recognized early literacy presenter, folk musician, and recording artist." Some of the resources you will find on this website include free downloadable poems suitable for each month of the year, free little books you can print out (basically one page that you cut and fold to make a book), fingerplays, action rhymes, and recipes: http://www.nellieedge.com/.
2. Speakaboos is a website where you can listen to online children's stories, such as Arthur, Curious George, and other classic stories. Story guides and worksheets are included for teachers to use: http://www.speakaboos.com.
3. The Preschool Express website created by Jean Warren has preschool activities, including songs, arts and crafts, and ideas: http://www.preschoolexpress.com.

IN the Library:

1. **Storytime**: Offer weekly storytime programs specifically for a local day care or Mother's Day Out center. These can be the same basic program as the library's regular storytime but open only to the center that is scheduled to come in that day. The library can schedule one day care a week if there are a number of day care centers in town or a weekly day care program for all the ones in the community if there is only one or two in town.
2. **Summer Reading Program**: Provide information about the Summer Reading Program to the local day care and Mother's Day Out centers. Hold one program a week during the Summer Reading Program designed for these groups and open only for them to attend.
3. **Literacy Kits**: Create or purchase literacy kits to be checked out by day care and Mother's Day Out centers. You can make your own kits and package them in bags, backpacks, or other containers. You can find kit resources by searching the Internet. Search terms include literacy kits, story sacks, story bags, literacy bags, literacy backpacks, and discovery packs.

OUT of the Library:

1. **Storytime**: Schedule a weekly or monthly storytime visit with each day care and/or Mother's Day Out center in town. The librarian or volunteer could do the same storytime program normally held in the library. Each visit a selection of books could be checked out and taken to the center to be read to the children until the next library visit. At the next visit, a new selection is given to the staff to use and the previous collection is returned to the library.
2. **Summer Reading Program:** An easy Summer Reading Program tie-in the library can do is to sign up the children in day care and Mother's Day Out for the Summer Reading Program. The center staff reads to the children each day for 15 or 30 minutes. A library staff or volunteer calls the participating centers to get the names of the children in the center for that day. The read-to time is recorded in each child's reading log. A library worker or volunteer takes reading incentives/prizes to the center for the staff to distribute to the children.
3. **Summer Reading Program:** Make copies of a little book or coloring sheet related to the theme of the Summer Reading Program to take to the centers each week of the program. These are given to the children and picked up at the end of the week by the library representative. The last week of the program each child's collection of little books are put in a small decorative white or colored box, and the children are given stickers to use to decorate their boxes. The children then take home their decorated box with their little books in it to keep.

as a family literacy program. Elements would be added to the program to model for the caretaker how to encourage a love of reading. In this case, the library would have identified and filled a specific need in the community.

2. The library's needs assessment revealed a large number of migrant workers with families. The assets assessment revealed the local health department was already providing health education programs to the teens in these migrant families. The library could partner with the health department to provide additional relevant programs.
3. The library learned teens in migrant families lacked home computers and had very limited access to computers during school hours. To help fill the need, the library could partner with the health department to recruit the teens the agency was already working with to take part in a library after-school homework program. Each teen would have uninterrupted use of one of the library's computers for a two-hour block of time.

Be open-minded as you consider the results of the assessment. Look at both the hard data you gathered and the opinions and impressions expressed in interviews and surveys. Be willing to change what you will do if unexpected information surfaces. You may discover the assumptions you had before gathering data were inaccurate or only partially correct. If this happens, you have an opportunity to create a plan that takes into consideration the new information by reconsidering potential partners, programs, or target groups. You might want to change where the program is held, how it is promoted, who presents the program, or when it is presented.

You might discover the library is not really the best entity to meet the need but one of the agencies identified in the asset assessment just might be. In that case, the library could facilitate or support the agency in filling the need. It could offer to promote the program at the library and on the library's website by offering to create a bibliography on the topic or providing a display of relevant materials that could be checked out from the library.

When you are reviewing the data gathered, you need to keep it in context. By looking at the results in terms of the library's vision, mission, goals, and objectives, you can better determine what would be an appropriate response. Each potential new program or service should be considered in light of the library's stated focus.

Points to Include

For all potential programs:

- State the need.
- Describe the larger audience or target group the library wants to reach.
- Describe the specific segment of the target group the proposed program will serve.

- State an estimated number of potential participants.
- Describe the characteristics of the audience (age, gender, interest, where they live, transportation issues if any, best hours for a program, etc.).
- List potential partners based on your assets assessment.
- List available library resources that could contribute to the success of the program.

Measuring Success

You need to develop a way to evaluate the program. Many times this is seen as a chore or pointless busy work, and it can be one of these if it is not done correctly or if it is done for the wrong reasons. Evaluation should be seen as an integral component of the program itself. The evaluation process should help you answer the question, "Did we meet the need?"

To help you do this, you set objectives for the program that will help you evaluate whether the program was successful in fulfilling the purpose for which it was created. Then you devise ways to measure whether or not you met each objective. Two common measures used are outputs and outcomes.

Outputs are simply things that are counted; they are quantitative. How many people attended the program, how many programs were held, and how many items were circulated are examples of outputs.

Outcomes are qualitative. These are usually subjective and based on opinions, perceptions, and views. They might be anecdotal, either verbal comments or written ones on a feedback form. Outcomes describe how the individual participant benefited from the program or service. You can use surveys, evaluations, and interviews to gather this kind of data. It puts a human face on the numbers. Often this kind of measure starts with the following phrases:

- Attendees understand . . .
- Attendees know . . .
- Participants have increased knowledge . . .
- Participants have increased confidence . . .
- Participants are acknowledged for their participation and what they did . . .
- Participants have the opportunity to share . . .

The objectives you write should be designed to help you evaluate the program to determine the following:

- Was it successful? Did it adequately address the need? Did the partnership work well?
- Are there aspects that need to be changed, deleted, expanded, or added? Was it long enough or too long? Were the surroundings comfortable? Were unexpected problems encountered?

- Was it effective? Did the results justify the expenditures in time, money, and resources? Is there a more cost-effective way the need could be met?
- Should we do the program again?

The key to writing outputs and outcomes is to be clear about the purpose of the program—what you are trying to accomplish. With that firmly in mind, you can write meaningful objectives and identify appropriate outputs and outcomes to measure the program's impact.

Qualitative data can also help you promote the library to your community and administration. It is a way to show how the programs you do can improve the quality of life for participants. You can all probably think of examples from your own library related to this. The person who took a job skills class then came back and told you he got a job because of what he learned. Or perhaps there was someone who attended a program on social security and learned about a benefit that would help her disabled parent. These stories bring to life the value of the library to the community. When someone shares a story like this with you, write it up. A short, to-the-point paragraph is sufficient. Next, add it to your library's website or use it as part of a short article for your local newspaper. Put it in a handout or flyer about a similar upcoming program.

Detailed Action Plan

Once you have identified the need, the audience, and the program to address the need, you must develop a detailed plan to implement the program. This is where the action plan comes into play. Use Worksheet 4.4 (p. 70) along with the following steps to help you write an action plan for your outreach program.

Steps to Writing an Action Plan

1. **Identify the goal.** The goal should express a clear sense of direction, purpose, and aim. The goal focuses on the most important outcome to be achieved or the benefits to be derived from implementing the action plan. Picture the expected outcome of the goal. Determine what can be done to accomplish it; these will become your objectives. Consider what makes your goal measurable; use this information when writing your objectives. Identify what constraints you have, like limits on time, money, personnel, or other resources; these will influence the activities used to achieve the objectives. An example of a goal is: Promote a love of reading in young children.
2. **Identify objectives.** Write down one or two but no more than three objectives for the goal. Remember, these are specific statements of what you will do to reach your goal. Objectives basically express the strategy that will be used to achieve the goal. Examples of objectives are:

WORKSHEET 4.4. DETAILED ACTION PLAN

Write the action plan goals and objectives in the space provided. This is the goal(s) ***of the action plan itself*** and the objective(s) to meet the goal(s). This will help you stay focused when you are writing the detailed activities or tasks to meet the objective(s) for the action plan.

For example, if your outreach program is to have a game day for senior citizens, the action plan goal might read as follows: The library will offer a game day for senior citizens to provide a program that will contribute to their personal enrichment and enjoyment.

The action plan objective for that goal might be: The objective of the library is to offer a senior game day for two hours once a week to encourage senior citizens to use their mental faculties and to increase their physical activity by playing games such as dominoes, cards, Skip-Bo, and Wii games.

Action Plan Goal(s):

Action Plan Objective(s):

In the following Action Plan Grid, record the actions, activities, or tasks you need to do. Put them in order of what should be done first to achieve the objective for the goal. Record how you will measure and evaluate the results.

ACTION PLAN GRID

IMPLEMENTATION			EVALUATION	
Action What action, activity, or task needs to be done?	**Name and Date** Who will do it, and by what date will it be done?	**Resources Needed** How much time, money, materials, and personnel are needed?	**Measurement** How will progress be measured (#, % of participation or attendance)?	**Analysis** How and when will data be gathered and analyzed to determine success?

- Provide a weekly lap sit program for very young children and their parents.
- Provide a weekly storytime program for preschool children.

3. **Develop measurable indicators.** These indicators will help you evaluate the program and partnership. Remember that two basic types of measures are outcomes and outputs. Outcomes are qualitative, and outputs are quantitative. An example of an outcome is:
   - "Since we started coming to storytime, my son insists on picking out picture books to take home. He pretends to read the books to his little sister."

   An example of an output is:
   - Over the past 4 weeks, the library has had 4 storytime programs with a total of 125 children and 45 adults attending.

   Here is an example of ways to gather data. For this example, we will use a "one community, one book" program. The goal of the program is to get as many people as possible in the community to read the same book and discuss it. You might have discussion groups, a library wiki on the book, and perhaps a presentation about the literary or social importance of the book by a local educator. You might measure participation and number of postings on the wiki (quantitative/ outputs) as well as qualitative measures such as feedback forms, surveys, and actual content of the wiki postings. In addition, you would list the various partner organizations and evaluate the success of each partnership. You might do a survey before beginning the program on awareness of the library, its programs, and the library's website. You could do a follow-up survey after the completion of the one community, one book program to determine if the community had an increased awareness of, and appreciation for, the library.

   Refer to Worksheet 4.5 (pp. 72–73) for additional examples of output and outcome measures as well as a template you can use to evaluate your own programs. Worksheet 4.6 (pp. 74–78) provides sample evaluation forms that can be used as is or modified to gather outputs and outcomes.

4. **Write a list of activities or tasks.** Write down all the activities or tasks necessary to accomplish the objectives to meet the broader goal. Think of as many separate tasks as possible that will be needed, breaking them down into the smallest steps required to complete the activity. Activities are the ways and means by which objectives will be achieved and evaluated.

   Here is an example of a list of activities or tasks:
   - For the objective to provide a weekly storytime program for preschool children, the following are some of the activities or tasks that will be performed (not in order of priority of completion):

WORKSHEET 4.5. MEASURING OUTPUTS AND OUTCOMES

The following examples will help you to see the difference between output and outcome measures and also illustrate how to measure outputs and outcomes. You can adapt the examples to suit your own program needs using the template provided.

Example 1: Spanish Language Materials

The library has identified a need for Spanish language materials.

Goal: Maintain a current, quality collection of educational and recreational materials.

Objective: Provide library materials in Spanish of interest to the community's Hispanic population, and promote the materials to potential users.

How will success be measured?

Spanish-speaking patrons will report increased satisfaction in having library materials in Spanish (outcome). Number of Spanish-speaking residents getting a library card will increase (output). Circulation of materials in Spanish will increase (output).

Outputs

- Count the number of Spanish language materials purchased.
- Count the number of promotional materials distributed.
- Count the number of people attending the special event to showcase the new materials.
- Count the number of new cards issued at the special event.
- Keep circulation statistics of Spanish materials.

Outcomes

- Eighty percent of Spanish-speaking library users getting a library card will indicate they are new library users because of the addition of Spanish language materials at the library.
- Eighty percent of Spanish-speaking patrons attending library programs report they are using the new materials provided by the library.

Example 2: Improve Service to the Elderly

The library has identified a need for materials in alternative formats to serve senior citizens.

Goal: Promote a lifelong love of reading.

Objective: Provide library materials for older patrons in an easy-to-use format.

How will success be measured?

Older patrons will report increased satisfaction in having library materials in formats that are easier for them to use (outcome). Circulation in large print and books on CD will increase (output).

Outputs

- Count the number of large-print books and books on CD purchased.
- Count the number of promotional materials distributed.
- Keep circulation statistics of materials.

Outcomes

- Seventy-five percent of the older residents surveyed report satisfaction with the new materials.
- Seventy-five percent of elderly residents surveyed that have used the new materials report enhanced personal satisfaction directly related to the use of the large-print books and books on CDs.

(Continued)

WORKSHEET 4.5. MEASURING OUTPUTS AND OUTCOMES *(Continued)*
Identified Need:
Goal:
Objective:
Measures of Success • • •
Outputs • • •
Outcomes • • •

- Write a storytime plan for each program.
- Select books appropriate for storytime programs.
- Select fingerplay/action rhymes.
- Select songs.
- Select craft to be done after storytime.
- Write and distribute press release.
- Create list of media outlets for press release.
- Create and print a promotional flyer.
- Post flyers in high-traffic areas of the library.
- Create list of outlets to distribute and post flyer.
- Have volunteers take flyers to outlets identified.
- Have volunteers contact potential outlets for flyer to get permission to post.
- Purchase craft materials.

(Continued p. 79)

WORKSHEET 4.6. EVALUATION FORMS

The following sample evaluation forms are provided for you to use or modify as needed for your particular project. They are designed to help you measure outcomes.

Coffee & Conversation Program

Thank you for attending today's program!

Place an X under the number to tell us how much you liked the program.

	Yes 3	**It was okay** 2	**No** 1
1. The program was:			
fun.			
long enough.			
2. The coffee was:			
good.			
3. Because of the program I:			
will have a better day.			
know more about what is going on in the community.			

Anything else you want to say?

____

____

____

Program Date: ____________________

(Continued)

WORKSHEET 4.6. EVALUATION FORMS *(Continued)*

Computer Skills Workshop Evaluation Date: ____________

*Thank you for attending today's workshop! Please take a few minutes to complete the **Before** part of the evaluation form before we begin and the **After** part at the end of the workshop.*

Place an X or checkmark beneath the number that best represents your evaluation.

BEFORE the workshop, I would rate my understanding as:	**Yes** 1	**Some** 2	**No** 3
1. Understand how to use word processing software to write a résumé.			
2. Understand basic computer skills.			
3. Understand how to use e-mail.			

AFTER the workshop, I would rate my understanding as:	**Yes** 1	**Some** 2	**No** 3
1. Understand how to use word processing software to write a résumé.			
2. Understand basic computer skills.			
3. Understand how to use e-mail.			

	Yes 3	**Just Okay** 2	**No** 1
1. The program was:			
informative.			
long enough.			
2 The speaker was:			
interesting.			
clear.			
3. The handouts were:			
helpful.			
4. Because of the program I:			
can improve my life.			
will use the library to find more information.			

Anything else you want to say?

____

____

(Continued)

WORKSHEET 4.6. EVALUATION FORMS *(Continued)*

Book Club Program **Date:** ____________

Thank you for attending today's program! Please take a few minutes to give us your feedback and comments.

Place an X or checkmark beneath the number that best represents your evaluation.

GENERAL	Strongly Agree 5	4	3	2	Strongly Disagree 1
1. The program was:					
fun.					
long enough.					
2. Today's books were:					
interesting.					
on a topic I like to read about.					
genres I like to read.					
3. Refreshments were:					
tasty.					
4. The facility was:					
comfortable.					
5. Because of the program I:					
have connected with others with similar interest.					
have more interest in reading these books after hearing about them.					
6. Overall the program:					
was enjoyable.					
was worth my time.					
was long enough.					
was valuable.					
met or exceeded my expectations.					

Comments:

____

____

____

How did you hear about this program?

____

____

(Continued)

WORKSHEET 4.6. EVALUATION FORMS *(Continued)*

Family Reading Together Program

Thank you for attending today's program!

Place an X under the number to tell us how much you liked the program.

	It was great! 5	Really liked it 4	Liked most of it 3	It was okay 2	Didn't like it much 1
1. The program was:					
fun.					
2. Today's books were:					
interesting.					
something I might like to read.					
3. The food was:					
tasty.					
4. The craft was:					
fun.					
easy to do.					
5. Because of the program I:					
will read more with my child.					
check out books for my child at the library.					

Anything else you want to say?

____

____

____

Program At: ______________________

Program Date: ______________________

(Continued)

WORKSHEET 4.6. EVALUATION FORMS *(Continued)*

Program Name: ______________________________

Thank you for attending today's program!

Place an X under the number to tell us how much you liked the program.

	Yes 3	I don't know 2	No 1
1. The program was:			
informative.			
long enough.			
2. Today's topic was:			
interesting.			
something I can use in my own life.			
3. The speaker was:			
interesting.			
clear and precise.			
4. The food was:			
good.			
5. Because of the program I:			
can improve my life.			
will use the library to find more information.			

Anything else you want to say?

____

____

____

Additional programs or presenters you would like:

____

Today's Topic: ______________

Today's Date: ______________

- ○ Have a volunteer package craft materials into envelopes (one for each child).
- ○ Pull or purchase books appropriate for storytime programs.
- ○ Purchase added value props such as music CDs, puppets, flannel board, flannel board stories, flip chart, and markers.
- ○ Create a list of program topics.
- ○ Create a program booklet listing all the programs and topics for the next six months.

Activities include what is to be done, by whom, the date by which it is to be completed, and the resources that are needed. After creating the step-by-step list of what is to be done, add the person responsible, date to be done, and the money and materials needed.

5. **Analyze, prioritize, and simplify.** Look at your list of step-by-step tasks. Which ones are absolutely necessary? Delete any unnecessary ones.
6. **Organize your list.** Decide on the order of your action steps. For each action, what other steps should be completed before that action? Rearrange your actions into a sequence of ordered action steps. Look at your planned actions again. Can you simplify it even more?
7. **Monitor progress.** Review the plan and completion dates for the activities and objectives on a regular basis. Ask these questions:
   - Has the plan moved the library towards its goal?
   - Has it moved the library towards fulfilling its mission?
   - Has it moved the library towards its vision?
   - Based on the answers, adjust the outreach plan as necessary.

Appendix (Optional)

Once you have written your outreach plan, you may want to add supplemental material in an appendix to provide information on how you developed the plan. The following are components you may consider including:

- Survey Results compiled from any surveys you did
- Needs Compilation from Worksheet 3.5 (p. 44)
- Assets Compilation from Worksheet 3.7 (p. 47)

Do not forget to thank those people who have helped you. One of the keys to success is acknowledging people. In today's time-hungry world receiving a thank-you note shows you cared enough and appreciated what the person did enough to take the time to formally thank him or her. Worksheet 4.7 (p. 80) is a simple activity sheet designed to help you keep track of people to thank. These may include presenters; volunteers who helped before, during, or after the program; the person who designed publicity pieces; those who distributed or displayed publicity

WORKSHEET 4.7. THANK-YOU NOTE

Remember to thank people who have partnered with you on a program or project. A simple handwritten note takes little time and can mean a great deal to the recipient. After the program or project is completed, take a few minutes to identify the people you want to thank.

Program: ______________________ Date Held: ______________________

Whom do you want to thank?	What did they do?
Partner Organization, Agency, Volunteer Name: Address: City: State: Zip code: E-mail address: Telephone number:	
Partner Organization, Agency, Volunteer Name: Address: City: State: Zip code: E-mail address: Telephone number:	
Partner Organization, Agency, Volunteer Name: Address: City: State: Zip code: E-mail address: Telephone number:	
Partner Organization, Agency, Volunteer Name: Address: City: State: Zip code: E-mail address: Telephone number:	

pieces; businesses or organizations that gave in-kind donations; those who gave financial contributions; and groups or agencies that partnered with the library or those who supported the project in some other way.

With your outreach plan written and action plan in place, you are ready to implement your program. The work you have done will help ensure it is one responsive to the community. It will demonstrate in a concrete way that the library's priority is on providing services to the people and for the people, organizations, businesses, and institutions in the community.

Sources of Community and Library Data

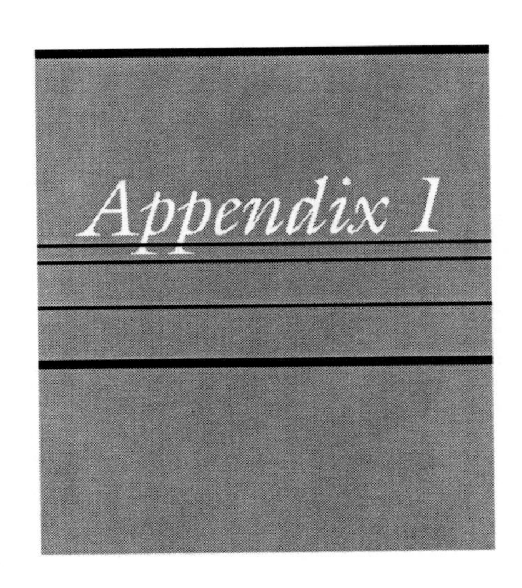

- USA County and City Statistics
  http://quickfacts.census.gov/qfd/index.html
  QuickFacts includes incorporated places with 25,000 or more inhabitants.
- American Community Survey
  http://www.census.gov/acs/www/
- Alabama: Alabama Library Information
  http://aplsnew-web.apls.state.al.us/libinfo/
- Alaska: Alaska Library Directory
  http://www.eed.state.ak.us/temp_lam_pages/library/dev/library_directory.cfm?category=A
- Arizona: Arizona Library Directory
  http://www.lib.az.us/LibDir/
- Arkansas: Academic and Public Libraries
  http://www.library.arkansas.gov/Pages/default.aspx
- California: Find a Public Library in California
  http://www.library.ca.gov/lds/docs/CaliforniaPublicLibraryDirectory.pdf
- Colorado: Directory of Colorado Libraries
  http://projects.aclin.org/directory/
- Connecticut: Connecticut Library Directory
  http://iconn.auto-graphics.com/staff/PublicLibraryDirectory.aspx
- Delaware: Find a Delaware Library
  http://www2.lib.udel.edu/dla/name.htm
- District of Columbia: Libraries in Your Neighborhood
  http://dclibrary.org/about/neighborhood
- Florida: Planning, Evaluation, and Statistics
  http://dlis.dos.state.fl.us/bld/research_office/BLD_Research_index.html
- Georgia: Library Directories
  http://www.georgialibraries.org/directories/

- Hawaii: Hawaii Library Locations
  http://www.librarieshawaii.org/locations/index.htm
- Idaho: Idaho Library Directory
  http://directory.lili.org/
- Illinois: Illinois Library Systems Directory
  http://www.cyberdriveillinois.com/departments/library/what_we_do/home.html
- Indiana: Indiana's Public Libraries
  http://www.in.gov/library/pldirectory.htm
- Iowa: Iowa Library Directories
  http://www.statelibraryofiowa.org/ld/c-d/directories
- Kansas: Kansas Public Library Services
  http://skyways.lib.ks.us/KSL/statistics/index.html
- Kentucky: Kentucky Public Library Directory
  http://www.kdla.ky.gov/directory.htm
- Louisiana: Library Directory
  http://www.state.lib.la.us/public-libraries/library-directory
- Maine: Find a Maine Library
  http://www.state.me.us/msl/findlibs.htm
- Maryland: Links to Maryland Public Libraries
  http://www.sailor.lib.md.us/links/
- Massachusetts: Massachusetts Library Directory
  http://mblc.state.ma.us/libraries/directory/index.php
- Michigan: Library of Michigan
  http://www.michigan.gov/mde/0,1607,7-140-54504---,00.html
- Minnesota: Libraries in Minnesota
  http://www.libraries.state.mn.us/about_libs_mn.html
- Mississippi: Mississippi Libraries Directory
  http://www.mlc.lib.ms.us/MSDirectory/PublicLibraries.html
- Missouri: Missouri Online Library List
  http://www.sos.mo.gov/library/molli/
- Montana: Montana Library Directory
  http://msl.mt.gov/For_Librarians/Library_Directory/default.asp
- Nebraska: Nebraska Library Directory
  http://www.nlc.state.ne.us/libraries/libdir/
- Nevada: Nevada Library Directory
  http://nsla.nevadaculture.org/index.php?option=com_content&view=article&id=547:nevada-library-directory&catid=85:development-services&Itemid=478
- New Hampshire: Library Directory
  http://pierce.state.nh.us/libdir/
- New Jersey: New Jersey Libraries and others of interest
  http://www.njstatelib.org/LDB/Reference/

- New Mexico: New Mexico Library Directory
  http://www.nmstatelibrary.org/directory/
- New York: Find Your Public Library in New York State
  http://www.nysl.nysed.gov/libdev/libs/publibs/
- North Carolina: North Carolina Public Libraries on the Web
  http://statelibrary.ncdcr.gov/library/publib.html
- North Dakota: North Dakota Library Directory
  http://www.library.nd.gov/publications/librarydirectory.pdf
- Ohio: Ohio Library Directories
  http://www.library.ohio.gov/LS/Directories
- Oklahoma: Directory of Oklahoma Public Libraries and Systems
  http://www.odl.state.ok.us/go/pl.asp
- Oregon: Oregon Libraries
  http://libdir.osl.state.or.us/
- Pennsylvania: Pennsylvania Library Directory
  http://www.libdir.ed.state.pa.us/Screens/wfLibrarySearch.aspx
- Rhode Island: Directory of LORI Libraries
  http://www.olis.ri.gov/libraries/directory.php
- South Carolina: South Carolina Libraries Directory
  http://www.statelibrary.sc.gov/sc-libraries-directory
- South Dakota: Libraries of South Dakota
  http://library.sd.gov/LIB/directory/index.aspx
- Tennessee: Tennessee Public Library Directory
  http://tn.gov/tsla/pld/
- Texas: Texas Public Library Statistics
  http://www.tsl.state.tx.us/ld/pubs/pls/
- Utah: Utah Public Library Directory
  http://library.utah.gov/directory/index.html
- Vermont: Vermont Library Directories
  http://libraries.vermont.gov/libraries/dir
- Virginia: Virginia Public Library Directory
  http://www.lva.virginia.gov/public/libraries.asp
- Washington: Libraries in Washington State
  http://www.sos.wa.gov/library/search/
- West Virginia: West Virginia Library Directory
  http://wvlc.lib.wv.us/html/libdirectory/alpha/viewallpublic.html
- Wisconsin: Wisconsin Library Directory
  http://dpi.wi.gov/pld/lib_dir.html
- Wyoming: Wyoming Libraries Directory
  http://www-wsl.state.wy.us/directory/

Examples of Community Outreach Plans

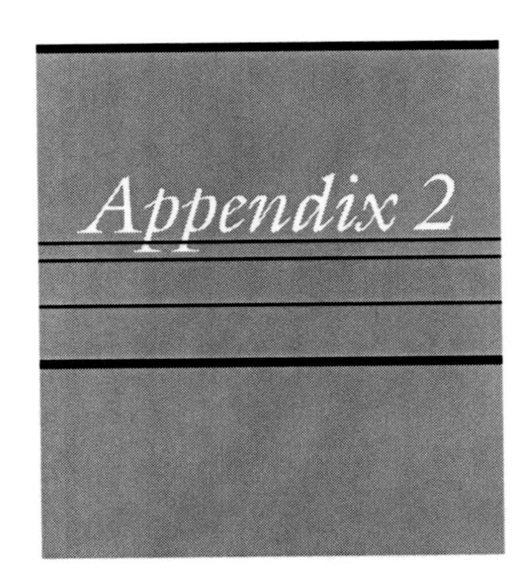

The companion CD-ROM contains the full text of seven excellent community outreach plans. The following list of contributing libraries also includes a brief description of each plan's goals.

- **Andrews County Library, Andrews, Texas**
  The library partnered with the local school, churches, and teachers (both active and retired) to provide an after-school tutoring program for elementary and middle school students.
- **Archer Public Library, Archer City, Texas**
  The library developed a weekly game day for senior citizens featuring Wii-type video games along with traditional board and card games.
- **Boyce Ditto Public Library, Mineral Wells, Texas**
  The outreach plan is designed to help the library develop partnerships with other organizations in the community to create a Local History Research Center at the library. The library and its partners will work together to collect local history materials, and the library will make the resources accessible and promote the center once it is established.
- **Muleshoe Area Public Library, Muleshoe, Texas**
  The library partnered with the Muleshoe Senior Citizen Center, Bailey County Aging Services, and the Dallas Region Social Security Office to provide a program on Social Security for local senior citizens.
- **Post Public Library, Post, Texas**
  The library is partnering with the local bookstore to hold an ongoing series of monthly book share programs. The programs are held in the Heritage House, a nearby facility that has a meeting room.
- **Yoakum County/Cecil Bickley Library, Denver City, Texas**
  The library is offering two series of early childhood literacy outreach programs designed for Spanish-speaking children and their parents. One series of programs is held at the Yoakum County Family Learning Center; the other series is held at the SHAPES Head Start Agency.

- **Yoakum County Public Library, Plains, Texas**
  The library is offering two separate series of programs for senior citizens. One is a weekly Coffee and Conversation program to provide senior citizens with an opportunity for socializing and networking. The other is a monthly informational program on topics of interest to seniors.

Bibliography

Books

Allen, A.A. 1987. *Library Services for Hispanic Children: A Guide for Public and School Librarians.* Phoenix, AZ: Oryx Press.

American Library Association. 1987. *Planning and Role Setting for Public Libraries: A Manual of Options and Procedures.* Chicago: American Library Association.

Baker, S.L. 2004. *The Responsive Public Library: How to Develop and Market a Winning Collection* [e-book]. Englewood, CO: Libraries Unlimited.

Baumann, S. 2011. *¡Hola Amigos! A Plan for Latino Outreach.* Santa Barbara, CA: Libraries Unlimited.

Best Practices of Public Library Information Technology Directors. 2005. New York: Primary Research.

Birge, L.E. 1979. *The Evolution of American Public Services to Adult Independent Learners.* Tempe: Arizona State University Press.

Brumley, R. 2004. *The Public Library Manager's Forms, Policies, and Procedures Handbook with CD-ROM.* New York: Neal-Schuman.

Carman, L.K. 2004. *Reaching Out to Religious Youth: A Guide to Services, Problems, and Collections.* Westport, CT: Libraries Unlimited.

Casey, G.M. 1984. *Library Services for the Aging.* Hamden, CT: Library Professional Publications.

Cassel, K.A. 1988. *Knowing Your Community and Its Needs.* Chicago: Library Administration and Management Association, American Library Association.

Cazayoux, V. 1967. *Public Library Services and Their Use by Professional Staff of Welfare Agencies.* Madison: University of Wisconsin Library School.

Childers, T. 1984. *Information and Referral: Public Libraries.* Norwood, NJ: Ablex Publishing Corp.

Coblentz, K. 2003. *The New York Public Library's Home Library System.* Philadelphia, PA: Running Press.

Davies, D.W. 1974. Public *Libraries as Culture and Social Centers: The Origin of the Concept.* Metuchen, NJ: Scarecrow Press.

Davis, D., J.C. Bertot, C.R. McClure, and L. Clark. 2009. *Libraries Connect Communities 3: Public Library Funding and Technology Access Study.* Chicago: American Library Association.

De Rosa, C., and J. Johnson. 2008. *From Awareness to Funding: A Study of Library Support in America: A Report to the OCLC Membership.* Dublin, OH: OCLC.

———. 2011. *Geek the Library: A Community Awareness Campaign: A Report to the OCLC Membership*. Dublin, OH: OCLC.

———. 2011. *Perceptions of Libraries, 2010: Context and Community: A Report to the OCLC Membership*. Dublin, OH: OCLC.

Dilger-Hill, J., and E. MacCreaigh. 2010. *On the Road with Outreach: Mobile Library Services*. Santa Barbara, CA: Libraries Unlimited.

Dowlin, K. 2008. *Getting the Money: How to Succeed in Fundraising for Public and Nonprofit Libraries*. Westport, CT: Libraries Unlimited.

Edwards, K. 2004. *Teen Library Events: A Month-by-Month Guide*. Westport, CT: Greenwood Publishing Group.

Fox, B.W. 1988. *The Dynamic Community Library: Creative, Practical, and Inexpensive Ideas for the Director*. Chicago: American Library Association.

Gervasi, A. 1988. *Handbook for Small, Rural, and Emerging Public Libraries*. Phoenix, AZ: Oryx Press.

Greiner, J.M. 2004. *Exemplary Public Libraries: Lessons in Leadership, Management, and Service*. Westport, CT: Greenwood Publishing Group.

Hanna, P.B. 1978. *People Make It Happen: The Possibilities of Outreach in Every Phase of Public Library Service*. Metuchen, NJ: Scarecrow Press.

Hennen, T.J. 2004. *Hennen's Public Library Planner: A Manual and Interactive CD-ROM*. New York: Neal-Schuman.

Herring, M.Y. 2004. *Raising Funds with Friends Groups: A How-To-Do-It Manual for Librarians*. New York: Neal-Schuman.

Josey, E.J. 1987. *Libraries, Coalitions, and the Public Good*. New York: Neal-Schuman.

Kim, C.H. 1987. *Public Library Users: A Market Research Handbook*. Metuchen, NJ: Scarecrow Press.

Kladder, J. 2003. *Story Hour: 55 Preschool Programs for Public Libraries*. Jefferson, NC: McFarland & Co.

Landau, H.B. 2008. *The Small Public Library Survival Guide: Thriving on Less*. Chicago: American Library Association.

Lynch, M.J. 1988. *Non-tax Sources of Revenue for Public Libraries*. Chicago: American Library Association, Office for Research.

MacDonald, M.R. 1988. *Booksharing: 101 Programs to Use with Preschoolers*. Hamden, CT: Library Professional Publications.

Manley, W. 1982. *Snowballs in the Bookdrop: Talking It over with the Library's Community*. Hamden, CT: Library Professional Publications.

Matthews, J.R. 2003. *Measuring for Results: The Dimension of Public Library Effectiveness*. Westport, CT: Libraries Unlimited.

Mayo, D. 2005. *Technology for Results: Developing Service-Based Plans*. Chicago: American Library Association.

McCook, K. 2000. *A Place at the Table: Participating in Community Building*. Chicago: American Library Association.

Monat, W.R. 1967. *The Public Library and Its Community: A Study of the Impact of Library Service in Five Pennsylvania Cities*. University Park: Institute of Public Administration, Pennsylvania State University.

Moore, M. 1995. *Creating Public Value: Strategic Management in Government*. Cambridge, MA: Harvard University Press.

Nauratil, M.J. 1985. *Public Libraries and Nontraditional Clienteles: The Politics of Special Services*. Westport, CT: Greenwood Press.

Nyren, D. 1970. *Community Service: Innovations in Outreach at Brooklyn Public Library*. Chicago: American Library Association.

Osborne, R. 2004. *From Outreach to Equity: Innovative Models of Library Policy and Practice*. Chicago: American Library Association.

Public Library Association. 1985. *Job and Career Information Centers for Public Libraries: A Step-by-Step Manual.* Chicago: American Library Association.

Robbins, J. 1975. *Citizen Participation and Public Library Policy.* Metuchen, NJ: Scarecrow Press.

Ryder, J. 2004. *Can't Get to the Library? A Directory of Public Library Services in the United Kingdom to People in Their Own Homes.* Surrey, UK: Julie Ryder Associates.

Seymour, W.N. 1980. *The Changing Role of Public Libraries: Background Papers from the White House Conference.* Metuchen, NJ: Scarecrow Press.

Shavit, D. 1986. *The Politics of Public Librarianship.* New York: Greenwood Press.

Smallwood, C. 2010. *Librarians as Community Partners: An Outreach Handbook.* Chicago: American Library Association.

Soules, G. 1975. *What People Want in a Library.* Vancouver: Gordon Soules Economic and Marketing Research.

U.S. Department of Agriculture, Rural Development. 2009. *Partners in Value: Value-Added Producer Grants: Building a Stronger Rural Economy through Value-Added Business.* Washington, DC: USDA, Rural Development.

Young, D. 1981. *Serving Children in Small Public Libraries.* Chicago: Library Administration and Management Association, American Library Association.

Zweizig, D. 1982. *Output Measures for Public Libraries: A Manual of Standardization Procedures.* Chicago: American Library Association.

Theses

Bossaller, J. 2008. *A Phenomenological Study of New Adult Readers' Participation in a Community Reading Program.* Doctoral dissertation, University of Missouri, Columbia.

Bretz, C.R. 2000. *Homeschoolers and the Mebane Public Library: A Case Study.* Doctoral dissertation, University of North Carolina, Chapel Hill.

Daurio, P. 2010. *A Library and Its Community: Exploring Perceptions of Collaboration.* Master's thesis, Portland State University, Portland, OR.

de Groot, J. 2009. *Building a Nation of Readers: Multiple Perspectives on Public Library Summer Reading Programs.* Doctoral dissertation, University of Alberta, Edmonton, Alberta, Canada.

Eanes, J. 2010. *The San Jose Joint Library: The Development of a Joint City/ University Library.* Master's thesis, San Jose State University, San Jose, CA.

Errickson, A. 1999. *A Journey into the Punk Subculture: Punk Outreach in Public Libraries.* Doctoral dissertation, University of North Carolina, Chapel Hill.

Heuertz, L. 2009. *Rural Libraries Building Communities.* Doctoral dissertation, University of Washington, Seattle.

Kelly, J.M. 2000. *Promoting Fiction: Readers' Advisory and the Use of Public Library Web Sites.* Doctoral dissertation, University of North Carolina, Chapel Hill.

Kenney, B. 2008. *The Transformative Library: A Narrative Inquiry into the Outcomes of Information Use.* Doctoral dissertation, University of North Texas, Denton, TX.

Kies, C.N. 1977. *Unofficial Relations, Personal Reliance, Information Influence, Communication, and the Library Staff: A Sociometric Investigation of Three Medium-Sized Public Libraries.* Doctoral dissertation, Columbia University, New York.

Lee, S. 2009. *Teen Space: Designed for Whom?* Doctoral dissertation, University of California, Los Angeles.

Most, L. 2009. *The Rural Public Library as Place in North Florida: A Case Study.* Doctoral dissertation, Florida State University, Tallahassee.

Rogers, J.E. 1977. *Information for the Urban Community: An Experimental Neighborhood Information Center.* Doctoral dissertation, Case Western Reserve University, Cleveland, OH.

Scharber Doering, C. 2009. *Online Book Clubs for the Net Generation.* Doctoral dissertation, University of Minnesota, Twin Cities.

Sin, S. 2009. *Structural and Individual Influences on Information Behavior: A National Study of Adolescents' Use of Public Libraries.* Doctoral dissertation, University of Wisconsin, Madison.

Smith, S. 2008. *Working Librarians' Perceptions of the Role of the Public Library in the 21st Century.* Doctoral dissertation, University of Texas at Arlington.

Articles

Amberg, P. 2010. "Where Angels Fear to Tread: A Nonlibrarian's View of the Sustainability of Rural Libraries." *APLIS* 23(1), 28–32.

Amirault, T. 2003. "It Takes an Entrepreneurial Spirit: Rural and Remote Library Service in Canada." *Feliciter* 49, 148–149.

Baker, J. 1987. "Rural Library Focus on Mission." *Public Libraries* 26, 58–59.

Barron, D.D. 1995. "Staffing Rural Public Libraries: The Need to Invest in Intellectual Capital." *Library Trends* 44, 77–87.

Bell, C.M. 2002. "Hablamos Espanol aqui!" *Alki* 18, 30–31.

Benstead, K., R. Spacey, and A. Goulding. 2004. "Changing Public Library Service Delivery to Rural Communities in England." *New Library World* 105, 400.

Blasingham, L., and S. Lawlor. 1998. "Rural Librarianship: A Bibliography." *Rural Libraries* 18, 44–48.

Bourke, C. 2005. "Public Libraries: Building Social Capital through Networking." *APLIS* 18(2), 71–75.

———. 2007. "Public Libraries: Partnerships, Funding, and Relevance." *APLIS* 20(3), 135–139.

———. 2007. "Working with Schools, Parents, and Other Community Groups." *APLIS* 20(2), 67–71.

Boyce, J.I., and B.R. Boyce. 1995. "Library Outreach Programs in Rural Areas." *Library Trends* 44, 112–128.

———. 2000. "Far from the Library: A Special Set of Challenges. *American Libraries* 31, 50–52.

Buchanan, W.E. 2008. "Volunteerism in Small and Rural Public Libraries in Pennsylvania." *Bookmobile and Outreach Services* 11(2), 37–58.

Burnett, J. 1985. "Small and Rural Libraries in Colorado." *Colorado Libraries* 11, 7–9.

Burr, J. 1985. "Library Service to Rural Youth." *Bookmark* 43, 115–117.

Campbell, S., and L.C. Dunn. 2008. "Marketing Teen Read Week." *Young Adult Library Services* 6(4), 24–26.

Canepi, K. 1997. "Information Access through Electronic Databases for Rural Public Libraries." *Rural Libraries* 17, 7–33.

Cannady, J. 1985. "Rolling Hills Mini-Libraries." *Show Me Libraries* 36, 15– 16.

Christenson, J. 1995. "Role of the Public Library Trustee." *Library Trends* 44, 63–76.

Cisler, S. 1995. "The Library and Wired Communities in Rural Areas." *Library Trends* 44, 176–189.

Clark, J.L. 1996. "Funding Sources for Rural Libraries." *Rural Libraries* 16, 22–40.

Colvin, G. 2004. "Community to Libraries in Caring: Reaching out to Rural Libraries." *Florida Libraries* 47, 13–15.

Dent, V.F. 2006. "Modeling the Rural Community Library." *New Library World* 107, 16–30.

Dezarn, L.M. 2008. "The Challenge of Latino Immigration for the Rural Library." *Bookmobile and Outreach Services* 11, 25–45.

Drake, D. 1990. "Library/LRC Service to Rural Extension Centers in Texas." *Community and Junior College Libraries* 7, 27–35.

Drescher, J.A. 1997. "Outreach and the Public Need." *Rural Libraries* 17, 43–50.

Durante, M.A. 1987. "Rural Medical Libraries." *Rural Libraries* 7, 1–26.

"Family Literacy Workshops Held." 1998. *Library of Congress Information Bulletin* 57, 282–283.

Farr, S. 2008. "Library Links in Lycoming County, Pennsylvania: A Cost-Effective Enhancement to Bookmobile Service." *Bookmobile and Outreach Services* 11(1), 9–23.

Fitzsimmons, J.J. 1996. "Librarianship Facing a Challenging Future." *Rural Libraries* 16, 35–47.

Flatley, R. 2001. "Rural Librarians and the Internet: A Survey of Usage, Attitudes, and Impact." *Rural Libraries* 21, 7–23.

Flatley, R., and A. Wyman. 2009. "Changes in Rural Libraries and Librarianship: A Comparative Survey." *Public Library Quarterly* 28(1), 24–39.

Fowler, D. 1989. "Rural Information Needs." *Rural Libraries* 9, 27–30.

Gerding, S.R. 2003. "Small Library, Big Fundraising: Community Support Is Way above Par." *Computers in Libraries* 23, 14–18.

Gilliken, P. 1982. "A Self-Supporting Library Service in a Rural Region: A New Look at Hospital Consortia." *Bulletin of the Medical Library Association* 70, 216–223.

Goddger-Hill, C. 1988. "The Realities of Collection Building in the Rural Public Library." *Rural Libraries* 8, 25–32.

"Great Reading En Route to America's Rural and Small Libraries." 2000. *Nebraska Library Association Quarterly* 31, 61–62.

Greishop, J.S., and P.R. Fretz. 1990. "Strategic Planning for Rural Libraries: A California Case." *Rural Libraries* 10, 45–60.

Hanks, G.D. 1990. "The Rural Environment's Effects on Library Service: A Consultant's Perspective." *Rural Libraries* 10, 7–24.

Hansen, E. 2002. "The New Kansas Library Card: Remote Access to Electronic Resources." *Rural Libraries* 22, 25–30.

Harris, K.D. 1999. "Lost and Found? Children in the Rural Library." *Rural Libraries* 19, 30–36.

Head, J.W. 1988. "Rural Libraries and State Library Agencies: A Study from the Center for the Study of Rural Librarianship." *Rural Libraries* 8, 7–18.

Hendricks, J.F. 1997. "Web TV in the Small Public Library." *Unabashed Librarian* 103, 7.

Hennen, T.J. 1986. "Attacking the Myths of Small Libraries: Ten Big Ideas for Small Libraries. A Center within a Center Helps Small Libraries." *American Libraries* 17, 830–832, 834–836.

———. 1986. "Conference-within-a-Conference: Rural Libraries Seen as Centers for Hope and Learning." *American Libraries* 17, 323.

Henry, S. 1988. "Tips to the Success of a Rural Children's Public Library." *Illinois Libraries* 70, 38–40.

Hildreth, S. 2007. "Rural Libraries: The Heart of Our Communities." *Public Libraries* 46, 7–11.

Hole, C. 1986. "Producing Quality Bookmobile Service without Going Broke." *Rural Libraries* 6, 19–30.

Holt, G.E. 1995. "Pathways to Tomorrow's Service: The Future of Rural Libraries." *Library Trends* 44, 190–215.

———. 2009. "A Viable Future for Small and Rural Libraries." *Public Library Quarterly* 28(4), 287–294.

Houlahan, J. 1984. "Three Types of Libraries Serve Rural Patrons." *Rural Libraries* 4, 63–69.

Houlahan, J.M. 1991. "Looking at Rural Libraries through Rose-Colored Glasses." *Wilson Library Bulletin* 65, 36–38+.

Howard, J.H. 1989. "The Role of the National Agricultural Library." *Rural Libraries* 9, 49–54.

Ingles, E., and A. Sivak. 2005. "Jasper Municipal Library." *Feliciter* 51, 154–156.

Ison, J.B. 1995. "Rural Public Libraries in Multitype Library Cooperatives." *Library Trends* 44, 129–151.

John, P. 1992. "How RIC (Rural Information Center) Provides Answers for Rural America." *Rural Libraries* 20, 27–38.

John, P.L. 1995. "The Rural Information Center Assists Local Communities." *Library Trends* 44, 152–175.

Jones, S. 2006. "Whitman County Farmers Reap Benefits of Library Services." *Alki* 22, 16–18.

Kernicky, G.G. 2006. "Modeling the Local Rural Library on the National Agriculture Library's Rural Information Center." *Rural Libraries* 26, 29–58.

Kirks, J. 2001. "When Does the Staff Find Time to Learn Things?" *Bookmobile and Outreach Services* 4, 33–46.

Klaiss, B.A. 1996. "Using Resource-Sharing Consortiums to Extend Automated Reference Resources to Rural and Small Libraries." *Current Studies in Librarianship* 20, 64–81.

Klevar, G., and M.A. Smith. 1988. "Rural Campaign on Illiteracy: The Region, the Technical Institutes, and the Libraries." *Rural Libraries* 8, 33–38.

Kniffel, L. 1996. "Rural Does Not Equal Underserved." *American Libraries* 27, 26.

LeClair, C. 1988. "The Library's Collection and the Rural Community: Some Possibilities." *Rural Libraries* 8, 30–64.

Loomis, R. 2000. "The Rural Web: An Outreach Service for Librarians from Librarians!" *Bookmobile and Outreach Services* 3, 12–21.

Lukenbill, W.B. 1995. "Providing HIV-AIDS Information for Rural Communities: A Role for the Rural Public Library." *Public Libraries* 34, 284–290.

Lynch, T. 1989. "Cooperation between Libraries and Extension." *Rural Libraries* 9, 97–103.

Marden, J.P. 1984. "Give Me a Home Where the Bookmobile Roam." *Rural Libraries* 4, 37–44.

Martin, I. 1984. "Stretching: Making a Little Money Go." *Rural Libraries* 4, 49–53.

Mazie, S.M., and L.M. Ghelfi. 1995. "Challenges of the Rural Environment in a Global Economy." *Library Trends* 44, 7–20.

McGowen, K. 2008. "Serving Migrant Agricultural Workers in the Rural Library." *Bookmobile and Outreach Services* 11, 47–61.

Merrifield, M.D. 1995. "The Funding of Rural Libraries." *Library Trends* 44, 49–62.

———. 1996. "And How Do We Pay for Public Libraries?" *Rural Libraries* 16, 23–34.

Minnick, M. 2001. "An Investigation of Library Services Offered to Kindergarten Students in Rural Public Schools in Washington County, Pennsylvania." *Rural Libraries* 21, 37–54.

Newhouse, A. 1984. "And Elsewhere in Nevada." *Rural Libraries* 4, 43–48.

"New Rural Library Powwow Draws 320 to Minnesota." 1984. *American Libraries* 15, 761–762.

Oak, K., and R. Gegg. 2008. "Increasing the Rural General Practitioners' Use of Library and Information Services through Publicity: A Randomized Controlled Trial in Cornwall, UK." *Health Information & Libraries Journal* 25(3), 208–217.

Patterson, L. 2002. "Tribal and Reservation Libraries." *Rural Libraries* 22, 19–24.

Pierce, J.B. 2004. "The Challenge of Starting a Rural Library." *American Libraries* 35, 77.

Preer, J.L. 1997. "The Wonderful World of Books: Librarians, Publishers, and Rural Readers." *Libraries and Culture* 32, 403–426.

Rawlins, S.M. 2000. "Rustic Roving: An Alternative Lifestyle Bookmobile." *Rural Libraries* 20, 63–64.

Reit, T. 2004. "Literary Lifeline for a Country's Rural Readers." *Farmers Weekly* 140, 63.

Riley, J.M. 1985. "Dragon Seeds: Programming for Children in Rural Libraries." *Rural Libraries* 5, 26–34.

Robb, E. 2010. "Gleaning Local History: Community-Based Digitization Experiences in Rural Washington." *Microform & Imaging Review* 39(1), 12–17.

Roberts, G. 2007. "Leading the Way: A Glimpse at the Role of Rural Librarianship in Nebraska." *Nebraska Library Association Quarterly* 38, 18–20.

Rosen, E.M. 1990. "Assessing Library Needs in Rural America." *Journal of Youth Services in Libraries* 4, 87–90.

Rothlisberg, A.P. 1995. "Sharing the Wealth: An Approach to Creative Professional Library Staffing in Northeastern Arizona." *Rural Libraries* 15, 21–23.

Roy, S. 1985. "Fewer People, Fewer Dollars, Fewer Services: Rural Libraries in Missouri." *Show Me Libraries* 36, 24–25.

"The Rural Library as Local History and Genealogy Center." 1999. *The Unabashed Librarian* 110, 12.

Salmon, R. 1999. "Growth and Vitality for the Small Library." *Rural Libraries* 19, 7–29.

Sanders, A. 1986. "Bookmobile Service in the East Albemarle Regional Library System." *Rural Libraries* 6, 31–39.

Sanders, R. 1989. "Libraries Alone: Down Under." *Wilson Library Bulletin* 63, 48–50, 52.

Saupp, K. 1997. "Connections: Internet in Rural Pennsylvania Libraries." *Rural Libraries* 17, 51–67.

Scales, A. 1986. "Manual on Literacy Programs for Public Libraries." *Rural Libraries* 6, 41–52.

Schmitt, J. 1990. "Cooperation and Rural Libraries." *Rural Libraries* 10, 7–30.

Sheller, R. 1985. "Reading Railroad, or the Search to Serve Children with Working Parents." *Rural Libraries* 5, 1–8.

Sisco, B.R., and D.L. Whitson. 1990. "Libraries: The People's University." *New Directions for Adult and Continuing Education* 47, 21–28.

Smith, C., K. Logsden, and M. Clark. 2005. "Consumer Health Information Services at Iowa City Public Library." *Library Trends* 53, 496–511.

Smith, S.M. 1999. "Why Telecommunications Technology Is Not Just an Option to Think about for Rural Economic Development." *Rural Libraries* 19, 6–20.

Snyder, T.A. 2004. "Rural Library Services to Minority Populations: Case Studies in the United States." *Rural Libraries* 24, 51–63.

Spencer, R.M. 2000. "The Rural Library in an Urban Environment: A Study of the Brown County Public Library." *Rural Libraries* 20, 7–32.

Starke, N.C. 1988. "Library Continuing Education Needs in Kansas: The Rural Perspective." *Rural Libraries* 8, 39–70.

Stephens, A.K., and K.D. Wright. 1990. "Planning Multitype Services in a Rural Environment." *Rural Libraries* 10, 25–44.

"A Survey of Rural Libraries and the Role of the Librarian." 2001. *The Unabashed Librarian* 119, 13–14.

Swan, J. 1996. "Automating Small Libraries." *Rural Libraries* 16, 7–22.

Tabor, J.M. 1985. "Developing a Rural Literacy Program." *Bookmark* 43, 197–200.

"Tapping into the Spirit of Community." 2001. *Illinois Library Association Reporter* 19, 1–3.

Trapp, J. 1999. "Networking Information Services to Support Local Business." *Rural Libraries* 19, 37–44.

Vasey, B.F. 1989. "The Intermountain Community Learning Information Services Project: A Participant's View." *Rural Libraries* 9, 105–107.

Vavrek, B.F. 1982. "The Future of Rural Libraries." *Rural Libraries* 2, 55–66.

———. 1985. "The Importance of Being Rural." *Rural Libraries* 5, 71–83.

———. 1985. "Rural Librarians: Geographically Separate but More than Equal." *Catholic Library World* 56, 419–422.

———. 1989. "The Rural Library: Some Recent Research." *Rural Libraries* 9, 85–95.

———. 1989. "Rural Library Service." *Wilson Library Bulletin* 63, 29–31, 34–38, 40–47.

———. 1990. "Rural Road Warriors." *Library Journal* 115, 56–57.

———. 1995. "Rural Information Needs and the Role of the Public Library." *Library Trends* 44, 21–48.

———. 1997. "A National Crisis No One Really Cares About." *American Libraries* 28, 37–38.

———. 2008. "Looking to the Future." *Bookmobile and Outreach Services* 11(2), 7–8.

Vondracek, R., and V. King. 2007. "Rural Libraries: The Strength of Community." *OLA Quarterly* 13, 1.

Walters, C.R. 1989. "OCLC and Rural Library Service." *Rural Libraries* 9, 69–83.

Walters, H., and J. Byers. 2007. "Current Statistics in Rural Librarianship." *Rural Libraries* 27, 25–29.

Walton, S.P. 2001. "Programming in Rural and Small Libraries: An Overview and Discussion." *Rural Libraries* 21, 7–23.

Walzer, N., and J.J. Gruidl. 1996. "The Role of Small Public Libraries in Community Economic Development." *Illinois Libraries* 78, 50–56.

———. 1997. "Rural Public Libraries and Community Economic Development." *Illinois Libraries* 79, 178–181.

Watkins, C. 1996. "Chapter Report: Rural Libraries and Universal Service." *American Libraries* 27, 9.

———. 2004. "Small Libraries, Big Ideas." *American Libraries* 35, 28–30.

Weaver, P. 1989. "Rural Information Needs as Seen by: Paul Weaver." *Rural Libraries* 9, 45–48.

Welling, P.H. 1996. "Introducing the Internet in a Rural Setting." *North Carolina Libraries* 54, 165–168.

Wendt, M. 2008. "YALSA's @ Your Library Advocacy Campaign." *Young Adult Library Services* 6(3), 10.

Whitney, L. 1985. "Folklore: Programming in the Rural Community." *Rural Libraries* 5, 35–62.

Wigg, R. 1995. "Across Towns and Across Times: Library Service to Young People in Rural Libraries." *Library Trends* 44, 88–111.

Willits, H.W., and K. Fern. 1991. "Rural Reading Behavior and Library Usage: Findings from a Pennsylvania Survey." *Rural Libraries* 11, 25–42.

Wilson, A. 1983. "A Marriage of Convenience—Or Necessity? The Combined School–Public Library." *Rural Libraries* 3, 75–94.

Wood, E. 2008. "When Distance Gets in the Way: Barriers to Recruitment in Rural and Remote Libraries." *Feliciter* 54, 54–56.

Wood, M.R. 2006. "Rural Libraries: A Story of Survival." *Alki* 22, 5–8.

Wyman, A. 2008. "Rural Libraries in Iceland." *Rural Libraries* 28, 21–30.

Yoho, J. 1997. "KCnet: A Rural Area Network Model." *Rural Libraries* 17, 7–24.

Zurinski, S. 2007. "The Impact of Small Community Libraries." *Texas Library Journal* 83, 126–127.

Index

O

P

Q

R

About the Authors

Barbara Blake has a long and varied career in the field of libraries and museums. She served as a public library director for 11 years; was administrator of a contemporary art museum; worked for the National Library of Medicine's South Central Regional Library Program where she coordinated the resource sharing activities of over 200 medical and hospital libraries in a 5-state region; worked for a regional library system providing consulting and continuing education for over 30 libraries; was a marketing representative for automated collection analysis with Amigos Bibliographic, Inc.; and was the project manager for the construction of a 15,680-square-foot library facility. She currently serves as Outreach Coordinator for the PEARL project at the University of North Texas. Among her extensive list of publications are *A Guide to Children's Books about Asian Americans* (England: Ashgate Publishing Co., 1995); *Bridging Cultures* (New York: Neal-Schuman, 1994 [with Tom Kruger]); *Creating Newsletters, Brochures, and Pamphlets* (New York: Neal-Schuman, 1992 [with Barbara L. Stein]), and "Cultural Diversity Resources" (Chapter 13), in *Children's Media Market Place*, 4th ed. (New York: Neal-Schuman, 1995).

Robert S. Martin is Professor Emeritus in the School of Library and Information Studies at Texas Woman's University, where he was Professor of Library Science and Lillian Bradshaw Endowed Chair until his retirement in 2008. Previously he served as Director of the Institute of Museum and Library Services and Director and Librarian of the Texas State Library and Archives Commission. He currently serves on the National Council on the Humanities and the Executive Board of the Urban Libraries Council. He has authored or edited numerous books and journal articles on library management, the history of libraries and librarianship, and the history of the exploration and mapping of the American West. His work has been recognized with numerous honors and awards, including Distinguished Service Awards from both the Texas Library Association and the Society of Southwest Archivists and the Justin Winsor Prize from the American Library Association. He is a Fellow of the Society of American Archivists and a Distinguished Alumnus of Rice University. In 2008 he was awarded the Presidential Citizens Medal, the second highest civilian honor conferred in the United States.

Yunfei Du is Associate Professor at the College of Information, University of North Texas. He teaches reference, technology, and management classes. His research interests include cultural diversity in library settings, community informatics, and cognitive styles. He is currently the principal investigator for the PEARL project, a research project working with rural libraries in Texas.

CPSIA information can be obtained at www.ICGtesting.com
Printed in the USA
LVOW091542200812

295135LV00010B/41/P

9 781555 707729